T0374994

ELIZABETH YARDLEY AND DAVID WILSON

FEMALE SERIAL KILLERS IN SOCIAL CONTEXT

Criminological institutionalism and the case of
Mary Ann Cotton

POLICY PRESS SHORTS RESEARCH

First published in Great Britain in 2015 by

Policy Press
University of Bristol
1-9 Old Park Hill
Bristol
BS2 8BB
UK
t: +44 (0)117 954 5940
pp-info@bristol.ac.uk
www.policypress.co.uk

North America office:
Policy Press
c/o The University of Chicago Press
1427 East 60th Street
Chicago, IL 60637, USA
t: +1 773 702 7700
f: +1 773 702 9756
sales@press.uchicago.edu
www.press.uchicago.edu

© Policy Press 2015

British Library Cataloguing in Publication Data
A catalogue record for this book is available from the British Library.

Library of Congress Cataloging-in-Publication Data
A catalog record for this book has been requested.

ISBN 978-1-4473-2645-8 (hardcover)
ISBN 978-1-4473-2647-2 (ePub)
ISBN 978-1-4473-2648-9 (Mobi)

Cover design by Andrew Corbett
Front cover: image kindly supplied by Getty

Contents

List of tables

Preface

This book is our attempt to push boundaries of theorising around female serial killers. We argue that existing literature is either too preoccupied with the individual at the expense of social context or too keen to identify the typical female serial killer to the detriment of nuance and heterogeneity. A new approach is needed, which acknowledges that each female perpetrator of serial homicide represents a complex combination of social roles and identities embedded within an overarching institutional configuration of family, economy, polity, religion and education. As such, we propose institutional mediation, an approach which considers the mediating role of institutions in terms of the nature and extent of their influence upon individual choices and actions. We illustrate this approach with reference to the case of Mary Ann Cotton and in so doing, highlight the importance of social and cultural factors in exploring how structure and agency come together to create opportunity. We believe that institutional mediation has relevance beyond the study of female serial killers and may prove fruitful for homicide studies in general because, while it takes a particular type of individual to commit homicide, it takes a particular social context to enable homicide to occur.

1
THE TROUBLE WITH FEMALE SERIAL KILLERS

Introduction

Since Jack the Ripper stalked the streets of London's Whitechapel in the 1880s, serial killers have become a staple topic for academics, the entertainment media and news media (Jewkes, 2004; Schmidt, 2005; Gibson, 2006; Jarvis, 2007; Haggerty, 2009). Furthermore, contemporary society has a fascination with serial homicide. However, despite capturing the attention of audiences and academics alike, defining exactly what we mean when we label someone as a *serial killer* is far from straightforward. In addition, distinguishing them from other types of killer, for example the mass murderer or the spree killer, has also proved difficult. Given the tendency of news media to misrepresent homicide (Maguire, 2002; Ferrell, 2005), it is not surprising that mediated representations of serial homicide are particularly distorted, fuelling an array of myths and stereotypes around this type of crime (Bonn, 2014). These factors combine to create challenges in grasping what serial homicide is, in both socio-anthropological and criminological terms. Even what would appear to be a relatively basic question – such as: Who are serial killers? – sometimes proves difficult to answer. To muddy the waters even further, we seem particularly troubled when it comes to describing, explaining and making sense of *women* who commit serial homicide, given the way in which such offenders challenge contemporary understandings of femininity and womanhood (Chan, 2001; Morrissey, 2003; Seal, 2010; Farrell et al, 2011). These issues will be explored within this chapter, drawing attention to the complexity that characterises understandings of serial homicide in general and female serial killers in particular. The chapter will also highlight the problems of current theorising when applied to the case that forms the subject of this book – that of 19th-century female serial killer Mary Ann Cotton.

Questions of definition

Defining serial killing is inherently problematic. There is no single agreed-upon definition used as standard within or across the various groups interested in serial homicide. Indicating the taken-for-granted way in which the term is used, while some writing on the topic clearly identify and justify the definition with which they are working, others fail to address questions of definition at all. Scholars falling into the former category have drawn on a range of criteria in formulating definitions, including but not limited to:

- the number of victims;
- the relationship (or lack of one) between the victims and the perpetrator;
- whether or not the perpetrator acts alone;
- the amount of time elapsed between killings;
- the period of time over which homicides take place.

To illustrate the considerable variation in the nature and extent of definitional criteria, the authors surveyed a sample of 20 scholarly contributions to the literature on serial homicide, noting the presence (and indeed the absence) of particular criteria across this body of work. The findings are displayed in Table 1.1.

The studies included in Table 1.1 apply between two and seven criteria in defining serial homicide. The most prevalent appeared to

Table 1.1: Criteria used in definitions of serial murder

Authors	Planning	Number of victims	Separation of killing events	Location of killings	Time between killings	Time overall	Sex of offender	Victim–offender relationship	Forensic or other links between murders	Single or multiple offenders	Context, i.e. civilian/military	Motive	Culpability
Adjorlolo and Chan (2014)		X	X			X			X	X		X	X
Bartol and Bartol (2004)		X	X			X				X			
Bonn (2014)		X	X		X								
Douglas et al (1992)		X	X	X	X							X	
Egger (1998)		X		X			X	X				X	
Farrell et al (2011)		X	X						X				
FBI (2008)		X	X				X	X		X			
Haggerty (2009)		X					X	X					
Harbort and Mokros (2001)	X	X								X			X
Hickey (1997)	X	X				X							

3

FEMALE SERIAL KILLERS IN SOCIAL CONTEXT

Authors	Planning	Number of victims	Separation of killing events	Location of killings	Time between killings	Time overall	Sex of offender	Victim–offender relationship	Forensic or other links between murders	Single or multiple offenders	Context, i.e. civilian/ military	Motive	Culpability
						Criteria included in definition							
Hickey (2006)		X				X	X					X	
Hickey (2012)						X	X						
Holmes and Holmes (2010)		X								X			
Homant and Kennedy (2014)		X			X					X			
Jenkins (1994)		X				X						X	
Keeney and Heide (1994)	X	X	X			X					X	X	X
Kraemer et al (2004)	X							X				X	X
Morton and McNamara (2005)	X	X	X		X					X			
Santtila et al (2008)		X	X		X				X	X			
Skrapec (2001)		X	X			X						X	

be the number of victims, appearing in 18 of the 20 studies, followed by the separate or discrete nature of killing events, which appeared in 10 studies. The overall time period over which killing takes place, the acknowledgement of single or multiple perpetrators and the motive for the killings were each included in eight of the studies. While this survey was a snapshot of studies with which the authors are familiar and by no means covered all research into serial homicide, it does highlight the considerable variability in both the nature and extent of criteria deployed in defining serial homicide.

The difficulty over definition raises several additional problems, one of which is establishing the prevalence of this type of crime (Ferguson et al, 2003; Hickey, 2006; Quinet, 2007). Differences in academic and law enforcement definitions can and do result in distortions of overrepresentation and underrepresentation. However, there is general agreement among scholars that, in relative terms, serial homicide is one of the most statistically rare types of crime (Jenkins, 1994). As well as overrepresentation and underrepresentation, *misrepresentation* also occurs given the conceptual disarray around definition, particularly when combined with media stereotypes. How then to distinguish serial homicide from other types of multiple homicide such as mass murder and spree killing? Definitions of these two subtypes of multiple homicide draw on similar criteria to that noted in Table 1.1 for serial homicide; however, a focus on particular factors does appear to distinguish them from each other. Mass murder emphasises spatial and temporal proximity of the killings – in other words, they tend to happen in the same time period at the same physical location (Dietz, 1986). Definitions of spree killing on the other hand are characterised by a greater degree of fragmentation – the killings may take place over a slightly longer period of time and victims may be targeted across a range of separate locations (Holmes and Holmes, 2001). What additionally sets mass and spree killing apart from serial homicide is that the former two do not include a 'cooling-off period', during which the offender returns to some semblance of a 'normal' life. Serial homicide is episodic and interrupted while mass murder and spree killing are continuous and contained.

The definition of a serial killer that the authors apply in this book is that which they have applied elsewhere – someone who has killed three or more victims in a period of greater than 30 days (Wilson and Yardley, 2013; Wilson et al, 2015). The authors employ this definition because it is effective in distinguishing serial from mass and spree killing, it specifies a number of victims consistent with other authoritative scholars, but is straightforward enough to be accessible beyond the academy, enabling a broader range of individuals to participate in debating this topic in the spirit of public criminology.

Of particular interest to the authors given the topic of this book were the definitions of serial homicide that made specific reference to the sex of the offender, of which there were only four. The question of sex is notable for its absence and by examining the definitions that do make note of this, we may be able to explore why this is the case. Both contributions by Hickey (2006, 2012) stress inclusivity, encompassing both male and female offenders. For Hickey (2006, 2012), the question of sex is an irrelevant one: it does not matter whether an offender is male or female – a serial killer is a serial killer going by the other criteria that Hickey's definition includes. However, an alternative view might be that sex is highly relevant, so relevant that it often does not warrant a mention. It can be argued that sex is a taken-for-granted characteristic, which would appear to apply when examining the definition proposed by Haggerty: 'a serial killer is someone who has killed three or more people who were previously unknown to *him*' (Haggerty, 2009, p 169, emphasis added). By way of further explanation, Haggerty includes the following rationale:

> The male pronoun is appropriate here as almost all instances of serial killing have involved male perpetrators. That said, some authors are uncomfortable with how women who kill sequentially have been effectively written out of the serial killer designation because they do not conform to the stranger-to-stranger dynamic....The sequential killing done by women, for example, typically involves killing people with whom they are familiar, if not intimate, including their own children, spouses

or, in the case of nurses, killing patients. Typically this intimacy with their victims means that they will not be designated as serial killers. (Haggerty, 2009, p 184)

Haggerty's exclusion of female serial killers is not particularly surprising. Holmes et al (1991) noted a general tendency among fellow scholars to exclude women from such studies and Schurman-Kauflin (2000, p 13) commented on the widespread disbelief that surrounds this type of crime: 'no one believes that a woman could kill multiple victims'. Indeed, amidst the development of serial killer offender profiling within the Federal Bureau of Investigation (FBI) during the mid-1990s, agents had simply one category for female perpetrators – the compliant victim – based on the assumption that the only circumstances in which a woman would participate in serial homicide would involve compliance, fear or stupidity (Pearson, 1997). All of this suggests that this is not simply about sex – the biological differences between men and women. Rather, theorising around female serial killers is underpinned by ideas around *gender*, the socially constructed expectations around how men and women should behave. This encompasses the central concepts of 'femininity' and 'masculinity' in how we *perform* gender in our presentations of self in society (Mead, 1934; Goffman, 1959; West and Zimmerman, 1987). The authors consider these observations in the next section, within which they explore the study of female serial killers and critically examine the theoretical and conceptual frameworks deployed in making sense of them.

Making sense of female serial killers

Studies suggest that around 15% of serial killers are female (Kelleher and Kelleher, 1998; Hickey, 2006, 2010). This underrepresentation of women is a reflection of broader trends in violent crime. For example, recent data for England and Wales reported that in 2012/13, 10% of homicide suspects were women and in 19% of all recorded violent incidents, the offender was female (ONS, 2014). Criminological insights into female serial killers are considerably less well developed than understandings of men who commit these types of crimes and it can be argued that this is attributable not solely to their smaller numbers but also to a historical lack of academic interest in female offending in general.

Academic enquiry into serial murder only appears to have emerged fully during the 1980s, growing out of Egger's (1984) seminal work. The study of serial murder today is characterised by the same lack of attention to female offenders that was a feature of enquiry into other types of crime over half a century ago. Feminist scholars began drawing our attention to women's absence from criminological theorising in the 1960s. Women's deviance was described as 'an obscure and largely ignored area of human behaviour' (Heidensohn, 1968, p 160). While enquiry into women's crime had taken place prior to this (Lombroso, 1875; Lombroso and Ferrero, 1885; Gibbens, 1957; Greenwald, 1958; Pollak, 1961), these studies abstracted female offenders from the social contexts in which they were located. As such, they did not acknowledge the potential contribution of women's social, political or economic discrimination towards their offending behaviour (Bouchier, 1983). Following Heidensohn's (1968) call to action, significant feminist work within criminology began to emerge and had gained significant momentum by the 1980s (Heidensohn, 1981, 1985; Morris and Gelsthorpe, 1981; Carlen, 1983, 1985, 1988; Carlen and Worrall, 1987), challenging women's 'invisibility' (Smart, 1976, p 178) and laying the foundations for the future of gendered insights into crime and deviance. It could be argued that from the late 1960s, feminist study within criminology grew in scope, nature and legitimacy (Miller, 2010). Despite this, some still argue that women occupy a marginal position in mainstream or 'malestream' criminology (Walklate, 2003; Sharp and Hefley, 2007) and it is therefore not surprising that insights into serial murder committed by women, an area of enquiry still very much in its infancy, is characterised by quietness or indeed absence. Therefore, if it is to be accepted that despite advances in recent years, women's deviance and criminality continue to occupy a peripheral position, it can be argued that academic insights into female serial killers are even more marginal. Indeed, it has been noted that '[c] urrent theory and research tends to place women in the role of victim rather than exploring the social constitution of female serial killers' (Thompson and Ricard, 2009, p 262).

In examining the literature around female serial killers, it becomes clear that there are three main types of academic contribution – the quantitative survey, the typology and the individual case study. Within the following sections, the authors will explore each of these in turn before applying this knowledge to Mary Ann Cotton, the female serial killer with whom this book is concerned.

The quantitative survey

This type of study analyses data from multiple cases of female-perpetrated serial homicide to generate insights about the *typical* female serial killer. This encompasses her socio-demographic characteristics and those of her victims as well as details about her crimes, including her method of killing, the number of victims, her relationship with them and the suggested motive for the killings.

The typical offender is described by Hickey (2006) as most often white (95%), with little or no criminal record and aged 31 at the time her killings commenced. A range of other studies support Hickey's observations and additionally suggest that female serial killers are educated caregivers who kill people who are socially or emotionally close to them through poisoning (Holmes et al, 1991; Wilson and Hilton, 1998; Scott, 2005; Farrell et al, 2011; Gurian, 2011; White and Lester, 2012; Farrell et al, 2013). In addition, some studies have explicitly identified mental ill-health issues or personality disorders among their samples (Keeney and Heide, 1994; Harrison et al, 2015). The larger study by Harrison et al (2015) ($N = 64$) in the United States (US) reinforced the findings of an earlier, smaller study (Keeney and Heide, 1994) ($N = 8$) in relation to histories of victimisation among female serial killers. Harrison et al (2015) found evidence of physical and/or sexual abuse in nearly one third of their sample, consisting of intra-familial abuse during childhood (14 cases) and abuse by intimate partners in adulthood (six cases). Harrison et al's (2015) study represents the most recent quantitative survey, from which they propose a description of the typical US female serial killer:

> She is likely White, has been married, and perhaps has had multiple marriages. She is probably in her 20s or 30s, and may be middle class, Christian, of average intelligence, and likely of average or above-average attractiveness. She is likely legally employed and may be a health-care worker or hold another stereotypically feminine job. She is likely in charge of caring for helpless others (children, patients). She may have been physically or sexually abused when she was younger, and she may have had issues with her parents (e.g. they were overly controlling or absent/deceased, mother was an alcoholic). She may have a history of conduct issues, sociopathological, or bizarre behaviour and may have a history of mental health issues. She may appear arrogant, while she may also appear withdrawn. She may engage in atypical sexual behaviour. She may have experienced a recent crisis, such as a relationship issue. Those familiar to her – even those related to her – are at risk, especially vulnerable individuals, e.g. children, ill, elderly. She may murder for money or power, most likely by poisoning or asphyxiating her victims – methods that mimic natural death – perhaps to avoid detection. She would likely kill in a suburban area. (Harrison et al, 2015, p 18)

Caution should be taken when examining these studies, as while some include only female serial killers acting alone, others combine solo female serial killers with those operating in teams, thought to represent around one third of all female serial killers (Hickey, 2002). This raises concerns over the extent to which such studies are valid. However, quantitative surveys are helpful in that they enable tentative comparisons with women who kill only once. This is an important exercise because it keeps the social and cultural context in mind and also heeds Hickey's (2010, p 255) advice to 'move beyond comparing women to men and compare women to women'.

Writing about the context of the United Kingdom (UK), Brookman (2005) argues that women who kill once do so within a domestic context and their victim is commonly their intimate male partner or their child. With regard to the sociodemographic characteristics of the perpetrator, they are often aged 25 to 40, with below-average educational attainment, unemployed and experiencing economic deprivation. Indeed, around 80% of the victims of female homicide offenders are members of their family, and 40 to 45% of women who kill, murder their own children, with about one third killing their male partner (D'Orban, 1990). Mann (1996) draws similar conclusions in relation to the US context, identifying the typical perpetrator as a single, African-American mother, aged 31 with a level of education below that of high-school.

Women who kill once tend to live in households where domestic abuse is entrenched, they may have childhood experiences of similar trauma, misuse drugs and/or alcohol, and they may lack formal and informal sources of support. Therefore it is not unreasonable to conclude, as Brookman (2005, p 181) did, that their circumstances are characterised by 'sheer desperation'. In killing a child or a partner, these women disrupt and confuse wider cultural views about who women are and how they should behave – their actions the antithesis of the carer or the nurturer (Chan, 2001; Morrissey, 2003). However, their violence is framed in a gendered way because we are able to cast them in the role of the victim. We reconcile the deviance of their actions with the emotional and dependent elements of feminised identity by arguing that they were driven to commit their crimes through helplessness and desperation. We make sense of their crimes as extreme but understandable reactions to circumstances in which their choices were restricted by the ways in which their gender had combined or *intersected* with other social factors. Such an interpretation enables us to make sense of some women who kill within our existing frames of reference around gender and femininity, effectively reclaiming them as women. While observers may be horrified by their crimes, they are reassured by their femininity and use that as a hook on which to hang their understandings of them.

From the findings of quantitative surveys, it becomes clear that female serial killers differ somewhat from the multiply disadvantaged women who kill once. While there seems to be some overlap in relation to age, mental ill-health and personal experiences of abuse and neglect, this is where the similarities end. It would appear that female serial killers draw from a wider victim pool, additionally encompassing those who are indeed dependent on them but outside of their immediate families. Furthermore, female serial killers seem to be less economically and educationally excluded, possessing somewhat higher levels of social capital than women who kill once. This presents considerable difficulty as it is challenging to convincingly conceptualise female serial killers as powerless in the same way that it is possible to do for other female killers. Some may indeed have been victimised during their lives but their position in the social structure appears less precarious. While they may have experienced disadvantage they are not *multiply* disadvantaged to the same degree as women who kill once. As such, they are assigned greater culpability and cast not as the powerless victim but as the evil monster (D'Cruze et al, 2006). Unable to re-feminise such women, the media roll out simplified, easily recognisable narratives into which to compress complex events and circumstances:

> A woman committing extreme violence can be presented as far more evil than a male killer. If she cannot be recuperated as a powerless, debilitated victim, the social threat that a murdering woman poses is often dealt with by 'outlawing' her symbolically from the social order through narrative strategies of demonization. (D'Cruze et al, 2006, p 48)

The typology

Typology has been a common feature of theorising around male-perpetrated serial murder (Hazelwood and Douglas, 1980; Holmes and De Burger, 1985, 1988; Dietz, 1986; Ressler et al, 1986; Rappaport, 1988; Ressler et al, 1988; Holmes and Holmes, 1996). Studies using typology attempt to categorise serial killers into specific groups according to motive and often refer to sociodemographic and other quantifiable characteristics thought to feature in particular types. To date, only Kelleher and Kelleher (1998) have produced a typology focused specifically on female serial killers. Holmes and Holmes (1994, 1998) also make a contribution to this field but their typology is built on an existing framework of male serial killers and, as such, may not fully acknowledge the gendered nature of women's violence (Farrell et al, 2013). Within Kelleher and Kelleher's (1998) typology are nine categories of female serial killer, based on their research into around 100 cases, half of which were from the US. Kelleher and Kelleher's impetus to develop the typology was rooted in their dissatisfaction with existing typologies of serial murder – notably the organised/disorganised dichotomy developed by the FBI's Robert Ressler and colleagues (Hazelwood and Douglas, 1980; Ressler et al, 1986, 1988). Kelleher and Kelleher's typology is summarised in Table 1.2.

As the only typology developed specifically for female serial killers, Kelleher and Kelleher's (1998) study is highly cited in academic enquiry in relation to this type of crime. However, female serial killers appear to be characterised by heterogeneity and, as such, as difficult to arrange into specific categories, a view shared by Farrell et al (2013, p 269), who argue that 'existing classification systems for these rare offenders are inadequate', including Kelleher and Kelleher's (1998) typology within this description. Indeed, they have highlighted several issues with the typology, which we outline below alongside our own reservations.

The descriptions and criteria for each of Kelleher and Kelleher's types are variable in that some include sociodemographic and other details – such as age ranges, offence-related information and length of killing periods – while others only include some of these variables. Related to this, establishing exactly what cases the typology was based on is challenging – nowhere do Kelleher and Kelleher provide a comprehensive breakdown of which women fall into which category (or categories – as the typology is clearly not mutually exclusive). A further key issue is that the typology builds on the idea of motive – focusing as a central point on why these women

Table 1.2: Kelleher and Kelleher's (1998) typology of female serial killers

Type	Description	Example
Black Widow	Kills multiple husbands, partners or other family members. May also kill victims outside of the family with whom she has a personal relationship. Begins killing after the age of 25. Kills for at least 10 years before being apprehended. Victim count: 6 to 13. Poisoning is her most common method. Motives are diverse and may encompass Profit or Crime.	***Belle Gunness:*** Active between 1896 and 1908. She committed her first homicide at age 37. It is estimated that she killed between 16 and 49 victims – husbands, children and workers. She used poison and killed most victims for life insurance proceeds or to obtain their assets.
Angel of Death	Kills physically vulnerable individuals who are involuntarily dependent on her care in an institutional setting (e.g. hospitals or nursing homes). Motives include a desire to control others and a need for recognition and self-aggrandisement through efforts to 'save' some victims. May have an undiagnosed psychological disorder (e.g. Münchausen syndrome by proxy). Kills adult victims by lethal injection of substances available in the workplace and may supplement this method with suffocation when killing children. Difficult to establish the number of victims given the normality of death in the killing environment but it is estimated that she will kill at least eight before being apprehended. Potential mobility between institutions may lead to a longer killing period or prevent detection altogether.	***Genene Jones:*** Active between 1978 and 1982. She committed her first homicide at age 27. She was responsible for at least 11 homicides – babies and children in her care while working as a nurse. She killed her victims through lethal injection (typically digoxin). Her motive is believed to be egotistical, involving elements of power and control.
Sexual Predator	Kills others in clear acts of sexual homicide. Motive is sexual in nature.[1]	***Aileen Wuornos:*** Active between 1989 and 1990. She committed her first homicide at age 33. She killed at least seven men while working as a prostitute in Florida. She shot her victims with a .22 pistol. Her motive is believed to be sexual – connected to her prostitution.
Revenge	Kills in revenge against an individual or entity. Killing is in response to an overwhelming sense of rejection or abandonment. Victims are symbolic of or responsible for her affront. Victims often include members of her own family. Poisons or suffocates victims. Kills three or four victims over a period of two years or less. Claims first victim when in her 20s. Rare – emotional characteristics relating to revenge do not often translate into sustainable aggression.	***Martha Ann Johnson:*** Active between 1977 and 1982. She committed her first homicide at age 22. Her victims were four of her children, all killed following arguments with her husband. She suffocated them by rolling onto them as they slept – she weighed around 17 stone.

1. THE TROUBLE WITH FEMALE SERIAL KILLERS

Type	Description	Example
Profit or Crime	Kills clearly for financial gain. Victims are not members of her own family. Driven by greed, killing is akin to a career to generate income beyond her needs. Organised, intelligent and resourceful. Aged over 25 when she commits her first murder. Claims between 5 and 10 victims during a killing period between 5 and 10 years. Poisons her victims. Likely to be apprehended sooner than the black widow as she kills in a local area – she is not a mobile killer.	***Dorothea Puente:*** Active between 1986 and 1988. She committed her first homicide at age 57. She killed individuals who lodged at her home and continued to obtain their social security benefits after they had died. She killed between 9 and 25 people, using poison as her weapon.
Team Killer	Systematically kills others or participates in their killings in conjunction with another person or people. Teams can be male/female, all female or family in composition. Female members are aged 20–25 when they commit their first killing, are active for one to two years (there tends to be an unstable relationship between partners) and claim between 9 and 15 victims. There is usually a dominant individual. Motives vary depending on team composition – e.g. male/female tends to be sexually motivated.	***Charlene Gallego:*** Active between 1978 and 1980. She was part of a killing team with her husband, Gerald. She was aged 22 at the time of the first homicide. The Gallegos killed 10 young women, whom they held hostage and sexually brutalised before bludgeoning or shooting them.
Question of Sanity	Kills others but is incapable of understanding the meaning or impact of her actions. Majority of these cases involve an Angel of Death serial killer. Rare because serial murder by its very nature involves calculation and planning – and therefore perpetrators are largely found to be fully culpable for their actions.	***Bobbie Sue Terrell:*** In 1984, Terrell is believed to have killed 12 people by lethal injection in a period of less than 2 weeks. She was 29 years of age at the time of the homicides. Her victims were older patients in the nursing home where she worked. She had a history of schizophrenia and Münchausen syndrome.

Note: [1] Kelleher and Kelleher (1998) describe features of the Aileen Wuornos case in relation to this type – as such they do not make further generalisations beyond the sexual motivation. They do, however, make reference to the case of Marti Enriquetta – a Spanish woman apprehended in 1912 for killing six children. She tortured and sexually abused her victims and engaged in acts of cannibalism with their bodies. The killings had a ritualistic element to them, involving boiling her victims' bodies in water.

Source: Adapted from Kelleher and Kelleher (1998, p 11)

committed serial homicide and using that as the starting point to build the typology. This may be problematic because of the gendered way in which understandings of women's crime are constructed, based on expectations of who women are and how they should behave, as noted previously in this chapter. To what extent is there certainty that socially constructed ideas about femininity and womanhood did not influence the formation of these categories, particularly since the process by which individuals were assigned to the categories is not explicated or transparent? As will be seen in the following section, Aileen Wuornos's label as a sexual predator is problematic, not least because she appears to be the only modern case in this category. In addition, the presence of an 'unexplained' category is also a cause for concern, both to the authors and Farrell et al (2013), who emphasise the vague and catch-all nature of such a category. Farrell et al attempted to apply Kelleher and Kelleher's typology to a sample of 70 female serial killers who were included in the original study, finding that in 56% of the homicides they re-analysed, the killings were driven by a combination of the Kelleher and Kelleher motives – a point they illustrate with reference to the crimes of Tillie Klimek:

> The crimes of Tillie Klimek exemplify the multiple motivations that can be attributed to a series of murders committed by a female offender. She profited from the deaths of her three husbands, which meets Kelleher and Kelleher's criteria for a Black Widow. However, profit accounted for motive in only three of the eight deaths to which she is connected. It is suspected that she murdered her boyfriend John Guszkowski after he attempted to terminate their relationship, and she was suspected of murdering the three children of an aunt with whom she had a disagreement. The murders of Guszkowski and the Zakrzewski children appear to have been motivated by revenge or anger, although Guszkowski's murder would be atypical of this classification because the offender murdered the object of her anger. Revenge was also cited as the motivation in the murder of Klimek's cousin Rose Chudzinskey when the offender poisoned her dinner following an argument. (Farrell et al, 2013, p 283)

All of this may suggest that focusing so heavily on motive may not be particularly fruitful in making sense of female serial killers. Indeed,

Farrell et al (2013, p 284) argue that 'these women, and their crimes, defy our need to label them and neatly classify their actions'. However, Farrell et al do suggest a starting point, which they emphasise will require further research:

> [I]t may be possible to broadly categorise female serial murderers into two groups, although this dichotomy may not be as applicable with male offenders. The occupational female serial murderer meets, targets, and gains access to her victims through her career, whereas the hearthside female serial murderer interacts and accesses victims through personal contact … Jane Toppan, Aileen Wuornos and Genene Jones would then fall within the parameters of occupational offenders, whereas offenders such as Judi Buenoano, Nannie Doss, Audrey Marie Hilley, Martha Johnson, Tillie Klimek, Louise Vermilyea and Stella Williamson would be considered hearthside offenders. (Farrell et al, 2013, p 285)

In identifying the social institutions of economy and family as the backdrop for their crimes through the suggested occupational and hearthside categories, and noting the gendered differential nature of men's and women's experiences, Farrell et al (2013) appear to be pushing this field of study into a more structural domain, moving away from simple description by emphasising the social, historical and cultural context of these crimes. The authors will return to this point later on in this chapter.

The individual case study

This type of study focuses solely on one female serial killer, exploring a wide range of phenomena in relation to her case. This may include:

- biographical themes around childhood;
- educational experiences;
- intimate relationships;

- critical incidents in her life.

It might also explore medical themes such as history of mental and physical health. While there is a plethora of literature from the genres of true crime and investigative journalism exploring female serial killers on an individual basis (see, for example, Schechter, 2003; Reynolds, 2004; Franklin, 2006; Phelps, 2011), scholarly contributions do not appear to be quite so plentiful. However, the academic literature that does exist sheds further light on themes that may prove fruitful in developing insights into female serial killers and questioning the assumptions generated from quantitative surveys and typologies. The authors include within this category their own previous work on Mary Ann Cotton, within which they considered a wide range of factors from personality disorder to Victorian cultural ideals of womanhood (Wilson, 2013; Wilson and Yardley, 2013).

It is not surprising that US serial killer Aileen Wuornos, who killed at least seven of her male clients during her time as a sex worker on the Florida highways between 1989 and 1990, has attracted the most scholarly attention in the form of the individual case study. Wuornos was anything but the quiet poisoner killing her intimates for profit that aforementioned studies have proposed as the 'typical' female serial killer. Acting alone, she shot her victims, who were strangers to her, with a .22 pistol. Wuornos killed *like a man* and was therefore difficult to reconcile with the caregiver and nurturer roles that permeated existing understanding of female serial killers. Her uniqueness could account for the inaccurate labelling of Wuornos by the FBI as America's first female serial killer (Hickey, 2002). Her divergence from an already highly deviant norm may also go some way to explaining scholarly attention to this extreme case study – intrinsically interesting because of its uniqueness (Yin, 2009). Individual case studies of Wuornos are of considerable academic interest in that they go beyond basic sociodemographics and raw descriptions of the killings. Considering Wuornos alongside team killers Charlene and Gerald Gallego, and Gwendolyn Graham and Catherine May Wood, Silvio et al (2006) question the labelling of Wuornos as a sexual predator, arguing that her crimes featured a strong profit and revenge motive, no evidence of sexual activity was found on her victims' bodies and she did not appear to have received any sexual gratification from the killings. Indeed, Silvio et al highlight Wuornos's history of victimisation, and as such re-feminise her to a degree: 'Aileen was abused by men her entire life and by shooting them, she was able to exact revenge for that abuse' (Silvio et al, 2006, p 255). Myers et al (2005) drew on their own evaluation of Wuornos shortly before her death and a range of documentation, including court transcripts, police reports, forensic pathology reports, forensic psychiatric reports, psychological reports and Department of Corrections staff observations. Like Silvio et al (2006), Myers et al (2005) also cast doubt on her label as a sexual predator and adopt a similar perspective to other scholarly analyses of her case (Arrigo and Griffin, 2004) in considering wider environmental and familial influences on her development:

> [T]here was no convincing evidence of sexual sadism in either her personal history or her method of committing serial murder.... The confluence of early childhood attachment disruptions, severe psychopathy, other personality disorder pathology, and a traumagenic abuse history likely contributed to her having serially murdered seven victims. (Myers et al, 2005, p 1)

Other individual case studies have focused on less-well-known female serial killers. Orstrosky-Solis et al (2008) describe their findings from a range of interviews and psychiatric and psychological tests with a Mexican female serial killer known only as 'JB'. JB was accused of murdering 12 older women and attempting to kill three more between 2003 and 2006. This study describes JB's impoverished and abnormal childhood, raised by a mother who was a heavy abuser of alcohol who 'traded her for three bottles of beer' (Orstrosky-Solis et al, 2008, p 1224) at the age of 12 to a man who sexually abused her for over a year. JB's abusive partnerships with other men are described in the paper as is her motherhood and her attempts to support herself financially through 'working on the streets selling candy and washing other people's clothing' (Orstrosky-Solis et al, 2008, p 1224). JB's involvement in professional wrestling is also described before going on to consider the murders and JB's explanation for them. The level of detail is evident in the discussion of the findings:

> [T]he question of JB's psychopathic traits has to be further considered. When arrested, JB confessed to having committed three murders, expressing slight feelings of remorse, and even posing to the cameras showing how she strangled her victims.... JB's social history revealed a diversity of potentially significant factors, such as: (i) her mother's alcohol abuse history and limited prenatal and postnatal care, (ii) physical, psychological and sexual abuse during childhood, (iii) lack of affective and social support, and (iv) extreme poverty....JB's general behaviour is governed by certain ethical principles. She can state what is socially correct and what is incorrect. (Orstrosky-Solis et al, 2008, p 1228)

Such rich description is echoed in Frei et al (2006), who focus on 'PK' – a European woman who killed two other women in 1991 and 1997 and attempted to kill several other individuals. Although by the authors' definition, PK is not a serial killer, the level of insight provided by a focus on her family history, personal history, history of prior offending and insights into her interactions with forensic psychiatric services enables a connectedness to the immediate backdrop to her crimes. Such studies enhance awareness of the particular social environments from which female serial killers emerge and enable us to reflect on how a combination of influences may have a bearing on the crimes they go on to commit. Perhaps most interestingly, in all of the individual case studies encountered so far, it is clear that the individual subjects did not neatly fit the description of a 'typical' female serial killer.

Mary Ann Cotton

Within this section, the authors introduce the case of Mary Ann Cotton, providing a summary of key details in relation to her life and the killings she is believed to have carried out. Thereafter, the authors draw on the insights into female serial killers generated from the quantitative survey, typology and individual case study to assess the extent to which current conceptual and theoretical frameworks are useful in understanding her case.

Introducing Mary Ann Cotton

Mary Ann Cotton (hereafter referred to as Mary Ann) is believed to have killed up to 21 people, many of whom were family members. Among her victims were three of her husbands, her lover Joseph Nattrass, her mother, sister-in-law, six of her own children and five step-children. She was born in 1832 in the small English pit village of Low Moorsley. Her father was killed in a pit accident in 1842 and her mother Margaret soon remarried another miner, George Stott. Mary Ann's childhood was characterised by frequent moves around the north-east of England as her father and later her stepfather pursued employment opportunities in the mining industry. Mary Ann was the eldest of three children, with a sister Margaret and brother Robert. Her family were Methodists and, as a teenager, Mary Ann taught a Sunday School class at the local Methodist chapel. Mary Ann's first paid employment was as a nursemaid to the Potter family, where she remained for three years.

In 1852 at the age of 20, Mary Ann married a 35-year-old labourer, William Mowbray. The couple moved to Cornwall but returned to north-east England some four years later with their child, Margaret Jane, who died soon after her baptism in 1857. The Mowbrays added further to their family and, by 1863, another two daughters had joined the brood – Isabella and a second Margaret Jane (named after her late sister) – as well as a son, John Robert. However, John Robert died in 1864 followed by his father in 1865; the cause of death in both cases included diarrhoea, a symptom of arsenic poisoning.

Mary Ann was therefore a widow after 12 years of marriage. Following Mowbray's death she received a £35 insurance payment and moved with her two surviving children – Isabella and Margaret

Jane – to Seaham Harbour in County Durham. Here she met Joseph Nattrass, who subsequently married another woman and moved away. Margaret Jane died in 1865 and her death certificate states that the cause of death was typhus fever. Isabella was taken in by Mary Ann's mother, Margaret Stott. Mary Ann was thus by herself and moved to Sunderland in the early summer of 1865, where she found employment in the Sunderland Infirmary. One of her patients was a single man, George Ward. On his discharge in 1865 he married Mary Ann, who became the main breadwinner as Ward was in receipt of poor relief, having been unable to return to work after his illness. No children came of this marriage. Ward died in October 1866, having puzzled doctors with symptoms similar to arsenic poisoning – his cause of death was listed as cholera and typhoid fever.

In November 1866, James Robinson, a shipwright at a small yard on the River Wear, advertised for a housekeeper to look after him and his five children, after the death of his wife. Robinson's three sisters had provided him with considerable support with the children during his widowhood but he felt that further assistance was needed. Mary Ann secured the job and within a matter of weeks, baby John Robinson died of gastric fever. By February 1867, Mary Ann was pregnant with Robinson's child, but she was called away to look after her mother. Margaret Stott was dead within nine days, the cause recorded as hepatitis, a condition sharing several symptoms with arsenic poisoning. Mary Ann returned to Robinson with her child Isabella, whom her mother had been looking after, and within a month two more of Robinson's children were dead, quickly followed by Isabella. All three children had been insured for small amounts of money and the cause of death was gastric fever. Mary Ann and Robinson married on 11 August 1867, by which time she was five months' pregnant. Their child – Mary Isabella – was born in November 1867, but was dead by February of the following year as a result of convulsions. However, the couple split because of disagreements over money – Robinson discovered that Mary Ann had been committing fraud and stealing from him – he then refused to take out life assurance on her request.

Robinson later moved in with his married sister and never spoke to his wife again, although they were not formally divorced.

After separating from Robinson, Mary Ann abandoned a new-born baby, George, with a friend, who in turn took the child to his father James Robinson – this child would be only one of two natural children to outlive his mother. Mary Ann was introduced to Frederick Cotton in early 1870 by his sister Margaret, with whom she had worked as a teenager for the Potter family. Frederick lived in the small, isolated mining community of North Walbottle in Tyne and Wear. Frederick's wife had died in December 1869 and Margaret had moved in to help care for his children. Mary Ann and Frederick soon began a relationship and by the end of March 1870, Margaret had died after experiencing severe stomach pains. When the Cottons were (bigamously) married in September 1870, Mary Ann was pregnant with Frederick's child, Robert Robson Cotton, who was born in January 1871. The couple moved to West Auckland in County Durham with their baby as well as two boys from Frederick's previous marriage: 10-year-old Frederick and seven-year-old Charles Edward. Frederick Cotton Senior died suddenly in September 1871 of typhoid and hepatitis and three months later Joseph Nattrass moved in as a lodger. Mary Ann had meanwhile been asked to nurse an excise officer known only as Mr Mann, who had contracted smallpox and they soon formed a relationship. As a result, there was talk of marriage and in the space of three weeks between March and April 1872, Frederick Cotton Junior, Robert Robson Cotton and Nattrass were all dead. The only person left in the household was seven-year-old Charles Edward.

Mary Ann approached Thomas Riley, a grocer and assistant overseer of poor relief. She requested that he take Charles Edward to the local workhouse as his presence was deterring a respectable lodger – whom Riley openly deduced was her new love interest, Mr Mann. He stated that he would do so only if Mary Ann herself were to enter the workhouse, which she refused to do. She then stated that the boy would 'go like all the rest of the Cotton family'. Riley took this to mean that Charles Edward would die and refuted Mary Ann's prediction, commenting on the child as a 'little healthy fellow'. On passing Mary Ann's house nearly a week later, Riley was informed that Charles Edward was dead, and with his suspicions raised, informed the police. Consequently, a chemical analysis was undertaken of the contents of Charles Edward's stomach, which demonstrated that the boy had died of arsenic poisoning. This finding would result in the exhumation of the bodies of other family members. At the time of her arrest on 18 July 1872, Cotton was pregnant with Mr Mann's child. Mary Ann gave birth to the child, a daughter, in prison and was executed in Durham Gaol in March 1873.

Making sense of Mary Ann

In revisiting the existing literature on female serial killers in relation to the case of Mary Ann, the crucial question the authors pose is: To what extent are existing insights into female serial killers helpful in making sense of Mary Ann? The most interesting questions were not so much concerned with *why* Mary Ann committed so many murders but how she got away with it for so long and how Victorian society made sense of her as a women who committed serial homicide.

In relation to quantitative surveys, Mary Ann did share some similarities with the 'typical' female serial killer. She embodied the quiet poisoner in her thirties, who drew on a victim pool encompassing members of her family and others who were dependent on her care. A further similarity is the difficulty experienced in trying to make sense of her within the victim narrative and the recourse to the 'evil' label described by D'Cruze et al (2006). The authors will return to this theme in later chapters but it is interesting for now to note how strongly this came through in mediated representations of Mary Ann in the Victorian press, seen here in an extract from *The Leeds Mercury*:

> A woman, still comparatively young, who has formed and enjoyed all the ties which are supposed to humanise the feelings and endear life, who has been a wife and a mother, and who never seems to have been suspected by friends and neighbours of being in any degree different from the vast majority of her sex, has

been proved guilty of the cold-blooded and deliberate murder of an innocent child. (*The Leeds Mercury*, 8 March 1873, p 7)

In relation to typology (Kelleher and Kelleher, 1998), Mary Ann would appear to fit into the Black Widow category in that she killed husbands, children, other family members and people outside of her family with whom she developed a personal relationship. Her murders also encompassed profit – she was the beneficiary of the various life insurance policies that came to fruition on the death of some (but not all) of her victims. Therefore, she could be conceptualised as both a Black Widow and a Profit/Crime killer. Turning to examine the categories suggested by Farrell et al (2013) – the occupational killer and the hearthside killer – it could be argued that Mary Ann was a combination of both. She could be described as an occupational serial killer as she met George Ward through her work as a nurse and James Robinson through her job as his housekeeper. She could also be described as a hearthside killer as she accessed other victims through her personal contact with them as their mother, stepmother, wife, lover and sister-in-law. Therefore, in relation to typology, Mary Ann can be assigned one or more labels, which may partially explain her motives. However, how useful is motive in explaining her actions? Many women may have had similar motives during the 19th century – a wish for more money and financial security – but very few of these women went on to systematically kill people to achieve this. Typology does not explain why Mary Ann acted on these motives while other women did not.

It is not particularly surprising that quantitative surveys and typologies are limited in their usefulness. They encompass women from a broad range of social contexts and periods of history. Aggregating them obscures the complex social realities of their lives, not least the cross-cultural and cross-temporal differences in gender roles and ideals of femininity that are central to understanding women's violence. As such, the individual case study may facilitate a deeper, richer appreciation of the circumstances and immediate environmental context from which Mary Ann emerged and generate meaningful insights into her lived experiences. However, such an emphasis on the individual does risk tipping the balance the other way in that it becomes preoccupied with individual psychology and biography at the expense of the broader social and cultural context. This problem of the micro over the macro is not a new one for the study of serial homicide. Nearly three decades ago the Canadian scholar Elliot Leyton argued that more attention should be paid to the bigger picture, that serial killers 'can only be fully understood as representing the logical extension of many of the central themes in their culture' (Leyton, 1986, p 10), a point echoed by one of the authors in emphasising the value of a structural approach (Wilson, 2009).

Returning to the question – To what extent are existing insights into female serial killers helpful in making sense of Mary Ann? – the authors would argue 'not very'. They are unable to shed light on why she got away with murder time and again. Most of what is known about female serial killers is descriptive, focusing on broad sociodemographics, typology and individual biography. The question of why particular women get away with serial homicide for so long has not been adequately answered and it is not possible to give a convincing response in relation to Mary Ann. There is a need to push theorising around female serial killers forward. Rather than trying to fit them into inherently problematic categories, a fresh approach is needed, which works from the bottom up. The individual case study is a promising place to start. After all, this approach does enable some reflection on how society makes sense of female serial killers but realistic efforts must also be made to contextualise any findings within a broader social and cultural framework. A neglect of the bigger picture in the existing literature has prevented consideration of the extent to which serial murder might be embedded within a gendered social context just as much as it might be rooted within the psychology of the individual. Within the next chapter a way forward is proposed.

2
INTERSECTIONS AND INSTITUTIONS: NEW PATHWAYS IN MAKING SENSE OF FEMALE SERIAL KILLERS

Introduction

Chapter One described the difficulties encountered in trying to make sense of female serial killers. Problems associated with the quantitative survey and the typology were noted. It was argued that in lumping together a large number of women from a diverse range of social and historical contexts to construct the 'typical' female serial killer, heterogeneity and nuance are lost. At the other end of the spectrum lies the individual case study, which, while rich in detail, is often abstracted from the wider social and cultural contexts in which female serial killers operate. It was suggested that a new approach is needed if better insight is to be developed into why women who kill serially are able to get away with murder for as long as Mary Ann did. This approach should be one that maintains a connectedness to the particularities of a case but enables reflection on both the overarching social structure and the female serial killer's engagement with this context. In this chapter, intersectionality and institutionalism are introduced, both of which encompass important considerations of relevance to this work. The authors begin by exploring the literature around intersectionality, which better helps to grasp the complexity of the social phenomena that they wanted to examine. Following on from this, the origins and varieties of institutionalism are explored and the endeavours of other criminologists in attempting to adopt an institutional approach are considered. Thereafter, the merits of such an approach in broadening understandings of female serial murder are explored.

Intersectionality: missing pieces in the puzzle of female serial murder

One of the key problems with existing theorising around female serial killers is, as noted above, the tendency of some scholars to aggregate all known female serial killers, obscuring their diversity. These women are being categorised based solely on their gender. This is a troubling issue given the existence of the various social divisions that shape lived experiences. Social divisions have been described as follows:

> … those substantial differences between people that run throughout our society. A social division has at least two categories, each of which has distinctive cultural and material features. In other words, one category is better positioned than the other, and has a better share of resources because it has greater power over the way our society is organised. (Payne, 2000, p 2)

This is clearly not limited to gender but encompasses social class, ethnicity, age, disability, sexuality and nationality, to name but a few (Payne, 2000). The female serial killers that appear in the lists and tables of quantitative surveys and typologies are not simply 'women'. They are individuals with social identities akin to patchwork quilts, featuring an array of social divisions – or sections – of varying colours and patterns, all of differing importance and significance. These features are far from separate – some sections overlap considerably and constitute central parts of social identity, others hang by a thread at the edges.

2. INTERSECTIONS AND INSTITUTIONS

This has been described much more eloquently by other scholars as *intersectionality*. Intersectionality appeared in feminist scholarship during the 1980s and 1990s (Burgess-Proctor, 2006), setting out to explore how 'class, gender and race (and age and sexuality) construct the normal and the deviant' (Daly and Stephens, 1995, p 193). In other words, this approach recognises that mechanisms of power such as race, class and gender do not act independently of each other in shaping life experiences but are overlapping and interdependent (Burgess-Proctor, 2006). While still occupying a relatively small proportion of the criminology literature, intersectionality is gaining momentum, particularly in an era of a 'backlash' against feminism and a need to prioritise not only gender but also its relationship with other key social divisions (Chesney-Lind, 2006).

In 2000, Britton argued that feminist criminology needed to progress from one-dimensional analysis (for example looking at gender but not social class) to embrace a multidimensional approach; exploring how social divisions intersect, interact and overlap. Indeed, such analyses had been quietly emerging prior to this and continued to do so thereafter (Maher, 1997; Wesley, 2006; Miller, 2001, 2002; Kruttschnitt and Carbone-Lopez, 2006). Perhaps most notable, however, was Potter's (2006) exploration of the intimate partner abuse of black women. This study drew attention to several intersecting components of identity – namely race, ethnicity, gender, class, nationality and sexuality – noting 'the Black woman is not one or the other at different places in her life but all components at all times' (Potter, 2006, p 120). However, Potter went further than previous work in addressing not only structural elements, but also agency-based micro-sociological processes: 'being oppressed and discriminated against based in any or all of these parts of the Black woman's identity can occur at the structural/societal level, within the Black community, and within interpersonal relationships' (Potter, 2006, p 120). This marked an important point in theory development as it opened up the possibility of exploring not only intersecting social divisions, but also their operationalisation at micro and macro social levels.

More recently, Bernard (2013), drawing on Merton (1968), has continued in Potter's footsteps by advocating understandings of intersectionality from the perspective of the individual offender: 'Having an understanding of an individual's specific desired goals and opportunities is therefore suggested as taking precedence over having knowledge of shared cultural goals and institutionalized means for success in explaining decisions to engage in criminal activity' (Bernard, 2013, p 3). The intersectional literature has therefore emphasised the importance of the interplay between social divisions such as gender, race and class and how these configurations are produced and reproduced within and between the micro and macro levels of society.

Intersectionality is of particular relevance because, with relatively few exceptions, serial killers are often discussed in terms of their individual biographies and personal characteristics, with scant or superficial attention paid to the social, historical and cultural backdrop of their crimes (Haggerty, 2009; Seal, 2010). They are studied within a vacuum that does not explore the wider local, regional and national contexts in which their crimes were committed. Therefore, the study of female serial killers stands to gain significantly from an intersectional approach as this not only moves enquiry beyond the individual to examine the social structure, but also examines the interface of the multiple social divisions that characterise that social structure. Having explored the studies around intersectionality, the authors were keen to embark on an analysis of Mary Ann that not only encompassed her gender but also explored the other social divisions that were a significant part of her social identity. In addition, the intersectional literature had made it clear that the interplay of social divisions is very much *experienced* by individual women as inequalities are produced and reproduced at micro and macro levels of society. This very much resonated with the authors' aims to explore Mary Ann's engagement with the wider social structures that formed the backdrop to her life and reflect on how she experienced them. However, how was this to be further developed? Several answers, as well as further questions, were found in the institutional literature, which are considered below.

From the intersectional to the institutional: towards a 'bigger picture'

While the literature discussed above clarified the importance of intersecting social divisions in women's offending, a robust framework was also required around which to build an approach to Mary Ann's case. It was clear that intersecting social divisions would be central to any approach adopted but this would need to be reinforced by a consideration of the social institutions that connect individuals to each other and the wider social structure. Indeed, as the authors had stated in earlier works, taking inspiration from Leyton (1986), 'serial killers like Cotton are not aberrations within their respective cultures – monsters from another time and place – but ... the very embodiment of the culture which they inhabit' (Wilson and Yardley, 2013, p 26). As such, the authors began to explore the potential of an institutional approach to Mary Ann's case.

The institutional approach – or *institutionalism* – focuses on the role of social institutions, which are defined as systems of rules governing the operation of social positions, the roles connected to them and the organisations in which roles are enacted and goals are achieved (Messner and Rosenfeld, 2004). Examples of such institutions include the economy, polity, religion, family and education. It is important, however, to identify what institutions are *not*: 'institutions are not to be confused with the organisations that constitute their concrete manifestation in social life' (Rosenfeld, 2011, p 12). Indeed, institutions are 'broader, deeper and more abstract than the organisations that comprise them' (Rosenfeld and Messner, 2011, p 127). Therefore, while a school might be called an 'institution' in everyday language, by definition it is an organisational manifestation of the institution of education. Messner and Rosenfeld identify three institutional dimensions:

- *structure* – the rules of the game;
- *regulation* – conformity with the rules of the game;

- *performance* – the extent to which adherence to or deviation from the rules results in particular outcomes (Messner and Rosenfeld, 2004; Messner et al, 2013).

While institutions were the subject of study by philosophers long before the establishment of social science as a discipline, the latter quarter of the 20th century saw political science embark on a critical exploration of the *new* institutionalism, which while not seamless, did claim the central goal of establishing the role and impact of institutions on social phenomena (Hall and Taylor, 1996). Three schools of thought, or institutionalisms, were identified: historical, rational choice and sociological (Hall and Taylor, 1996).

Historical institutionalism places particular emphasis on explaining the emergence of institutions and exploring their characteristics. This school of thought examines how institutions develop over time in being shaped by past events and responding to contemporary challenges. Historical institutionalism focuses largely on the macro level, not going into particular detail regarding the relationship between the structural institution and the individual agent or actor.

Rational choice institutionalism, on the other hand, does place a firm emphasis on actors within institutions. This school of thought is based on the premise that actors have a fixed set of preferences, wants and needs and will behave in a wholly instrumental way in seeking to meet them. Their actions are based on what they can deduce about the behaviour of other actors, with institutions providing the framework for such interactions 'by affecting the range and sequence of alternatives on the choice-agenda or by providing information and enforcement mechanisms that reduce uncertainty about the corresponding behaviour of others' (Hall and Taylor, 1996, p 945).

The approach adopted here most readily identifies with *sociological institutionalism*, which challenges rationalist Weberian conceptualisations of institutions and social action. Critiquing structural determinism, sociological institutionalism emphasises a dynamic relationship between individuals and institutions, characterised by co-construction and negotiation. As such, cultural components such as values, beliefs and norms are central to this approach (Meyer and Rowan, 1977; Brinton and Nee, 1998; Peters, 1999). Institutions reflect embedded cultural understandings and mirror power imbalances within social contexts (Thelen, 1999; Messner et al, 2013). In terms of the relationship between institutions and individual actors, Hall and Taylor (1996) suggest that institutions provide blueprints for social action:

> [W]hen faced with a situation, the individual must find a way of recognizing it as well as responding to it, and the scripts or templates implicit in the institutional world provide the means for accomplishing both of these tasks ... the individual works and reworks the available institutional templates to devise a course of action. (Hall and Taylor, 1996, pp 948-949)

Actors are guided by the logic of appropriateness (March and Olsen, 1989, 1998; Powell and DiMaggio, 1991), reconciling potential courses of action with mainstream standards of socially appropriate behaviour. Actors are rational, but this rationality is socially constructed, driven and constrained by social norms and expectations rather than individual instrumental goals (March and Olsen, 1989, 1998; Powell and DiMaggio, 1991; Fligstein, 1997; Brinton and Nee, 1998). Drawing on social psychology and cultural anthropology, other scholars recognise such processes as *frames* and *scripts*. 'Frames provide basic definitions of the situation ... scripts provide guidance about how to behave in a given situation defined in a particular way' (Kroneberg, 2006, p 10; Messner, 2012). In addition, as Hay and Wincott (1998, p 955) emphasise, knowledge of the institutional environment is not equally distributed and, as such, this 'affects the ability of actors to transform the contexts (institutional and otherwise) in which they find themselves'. Hall and Taylor (1998, p 961) reinforce this view: 'By showing how institutions confer power or authority on some actors while reducing the power of others ... institutionalists are, in some sense at least, explaining how institutions can be constitutive of political agency'. Therefore, in applying this approach to Mary Ann's case, there lies potential to begin to bridge the longstanding gap between structural and agency factors in exploring not only how an individual's engagement with the institutional frameworks within society is configured but also the extent to which they are able (or unable) to influence the nature of that relationship.

Criminology and institutionalism

Criminologists are well aware of the considerable potential of an institutionalist approach (Messner and Rosenfeld, 2004; Karstedt, 2010; Messner et al, 2013). Several have embarked on institutional studies and in so doing have made significant contributions to our understanding of a range of criminological phenomena. The relationship between crime rates and changes in social structure has been explored by LaFree (1998) and Messner and Rosenfeld (2007). Most recently, this has been addressed by Nivette (2014) in considering the effect of state legitimacy on levels of crime and violence. A number of other scholars have embarked on comparative studies of punishment (Garland, 1985, 2001; Cavadino and Dignan, 2006; Lacey, 2008). Focusing on women's criminality through historical institutionalism, Way (2004, p 90) identified the 'periodization loop' – recurrent time periods in which women are seen as objects for either rehabilitation or reform.

Further studies include those with a specific focus on the institutional context of homicide (Gartner, 1991; LaFree and Drass, 2002; Pridemore and Kim, 2007; Roth, 2009). Recent research by Nivette and Eisner (2013) explored state legitimacy as a predictor of homicide, arguing that states in which citizens demonstrate higher levels of acceptance of the state's authority are associated with lower levels of homicide. Focusing specifically on women as the victims of homicide, Gartner et al (1990) explored the hypothesis that changes in women's gender roles and statuses would have an impact on their risk of becoming homicide victims. Having analysed data from 18 nations over a 30-year period, Gartner et al (1990) found their proposition to be accurate, discovering that in countries where women had less traditional gender roles that went beyond a focus on the homemaker, there were higher victimisation rates but that this was conditional on women's status in relation to educational attainment. In other words, where women were better able to access post-compulsory education, this acted as a protective factor. Building on Gartner et al (1990), Stamatel (2014) analysed data from European countries over a 25-year period and came to similar conclusions, stating that better economic conditions tend to reduce victimisation. This study is of particular interest given Stamatel's plea for appreciation of the complexity that emerges when institutional studies begin to engage with questions of gender: 'understanding macro-level variations in female homicide victimization requires multifaceted explanations that bridge criminological theories and that are also sensitive to socio-historical context' (Stamatel, 2014, p 578).

Turning to examine homicide offenders, Pridemore's (2007) research on post-communist Russia suggested that the characteristics of perpetrators are sensitive to the social and political context. Pridemore discovered that homicide offender characteristics changed substantially between 1989–91 and 1998 and perhaps most interesting is the finding that while only about 1% of offenders were women in 1989–91, this had increased to 10% in 1998. By way of explanation, Pridemore comments on a general decline in women's social and economic wellbeing following the fall of communism, noting rising unemployment and increasing levels of stress within the home – in essence there were more women whose circumstances were characterised by the 'sheer desperation' (Brookman, 2005, p 181) typical of women who commit homicide once. Similarly, changes in social roles and statuses formed part of the explanation for increases in the proportion of female perpetrators of homicide in Chicago in a later study (Gruenewald and Pridemore, 2009).

Perhaps one of the best-known and most highly cited institutional contributions in criminology is institutional anomie theory (IAT) (Messner and Rosenfeld, 2007). Anomie refers to a state of normlessness in society, where the rules no longer apply:

It refers to a breakdown of social standards governing behavior and so also signifies little social cohesion. When a high degree

of anomie has set in, the rules once governing conduct have
lost their savor and their force. Above all else, they are deprived
of legitimacy. (Merton, 1964, p 226)

As such, the rules that keep people on the straight and narrow are no
longer effective in maintaining social order and harmony and crime
is an inevitable consequence. IAT sets itself the task of identifying
what type of institutional arrangements facilitate anomie – what does
the social structure 'look like' when this type of disorder emerges?
This clearly involves examining the nature of key social institutions –
economy, polity, religion, education and family. The central premise of
IAT focuses on the role of the economy in advanced societies, claiming
that where the norms and roles of economy are prioritised, high levels
of crime are likely. Essentially, in such societies, the economy has taken
precedence – other social institutions are devalued and saturated with
economic ideology as actors prioritise their economic roles over those
in other institutions. IAT proponents argue that this can result in
significant harms because in such a situation, the role of non-economic
institutions such as the family and religion in providing actors with a
moral and ethical education is compromised (Messner and Rosenfeld,
2007). In addition, the dominance of the economy not only hinders
these institutions in fulfilling this role but also replaces moral and
ethical education with economic education – whereby individuals
become over-socialised or 'hypersocialised' (Messner, 2012, p 12) into
economic ideologies, accepting the primacy of the market as normal
and right and resorting to criminality to achieve economic outcomes.
  In the same way that feminist scholars expressed concern over the
gendered nature of Merton's anomie and its tendency to treat men as
normative (Leonard, 1983), theorists have emphasised the need for
gender sensitivity in IAT, arguing that women and gender should not
be seen as exceptions or add-ons, but central to the theory (Applin
and Messner, 2015). This work has significant overlaps with that cited
earlier in relation to intersectionality, arguing that gender is not simply
a sociodemographic variable but an inherent part of social identity,
'embedded in the very *structure* of institutions that are built and

maintained on gendered ideology and symbolism, and populated by gendered actors who have differential rates of institutional participation' (Applin and Messner, 2015, p 41, emphasis in original). Applin and Messner (2015) consider the social roles connected to the family and the economy in contemporary society, emphasising the demands of both institutions and the tendency for men to sacrifice family roles to accommodate economic roles while women are less able to do so given the inherently gendered and feminised nature of family roles. As such, Applin and Messner (2015) draw attention to the importance of gender in micro-level manifestations of macro-level structural arrangements.

From exploring the institutional literature, several important points emerged. First, sociological institutionalism has been a promising epistemological approach because it recognises the interplay between structure and agency. Second, sociological institutionalism provide a starting point for further exploring this relationship by noting the presence of blueprints (or frames) and logics of appropriateness (or scripts) through which actors develop a course of action. Third, developments in IAT have recently emphasised the importance of gender in such a way that suggests that institutional and intersectional approaches could be complementary and fruitful. In addition, institutional studies of homicide have established the centrality of social roles in explaining both women's victimisation and female-perpetrated homicide, which suggests that social roles should be an important component of the approach developed for studying Mary Ann. However, given the macro orientation towards exploring quantitative data, institutional homicide research has not engaged in the study of individual actors. While they have indeed referred to the impact of institutional arrangements on actors in general, they have not looked at specific individual actors nor considered the significance of intersecting social divisions on those actors' lived experiences. As such, these studies are largely characteristic of historical and rational choice institutionalism rather than sociological institutionalism. So while criminologists have indeed adopted an institutional approach to homicide and addressed the issue of gender within this, questions focused on specific actors with distinct intersectional identities and unique relationships with the institutional structure remain both unasked and unanswered.

A new route towards understanding female serial killers

Looking back at the literature on serial murder in general and female serial killers in particular, it becomes clear that current academic insights are limited for two reasons. First, there is a preoccupation with the development of typology, which goes hand in hand with quantitative surveys, identifying and categorising clusters of characteristics and positing a 'typical' female serial killer. Second, other scholarly endeavours are characteristic of the micro criminological approach, which focuses on the individual offender's psychology and biography at the expense of the broader social context or 'bigger picture' (Haggerty, 2009; Rosenfeld, 2011). The social contexts of individual female serial killers therefore remain uncharted, the structures within which their crimes took place unexplored and their role in creating the conditions in which serial murder occurred unexamined. While a small number of criminologists, the authors included, have acknowledged the importance of social context in understanding women who kill (D'Cruze et al, 2006; Seal, 2010; Wilson, 2013; Wilson and Yardley, 2013), they have not yet developed a theoretically informed or systematic method for analysing the social context of female serial murder and as such the gap between the micro and the macro remains.

The study of female serial killers is characteristic of the 'epistemological imbalance' (Messner, 2012, p 6) in criminology, whereby scholars engaged with micro phenomena are preoccupied with detail at the expense of context and those who study macro-level phenomena do not sufficiently explain its impact at the micro level. Messner's call to action encouraged the authors in their efforts to develop such work, taking inspiration from the institutional approach. However, institutional theory has been typically used to explain overall conformity and aggregate levels of crime, whereas the authors were planning to explain one case of extreme, individual deviance.

Therefore, while key concepts were borrowed from institutionalism – notably 'institutional configurations' and 'social roles' – the study would differ from the positivist historical and rational choice institutionalism that underpins existing institutional studies of homicide. The focus is not on institutional structures but a structurally embedded individual. So while the study of Mary Ann here clearly involves a description and explanation of the institutional configurations of the Victorian society she inhabited and the gendered nature of such arrangements, enquiry does not stop there. The authors wish to consider Mary Ann's positioning within these structures and explore her lived experience through the evidence available, and this desire inevitably involves epistemology that is distinctly anti-positivist in flavour, attempting to glean insights into Mary Ann's subjectivity (Burrell and Morgan, 1979).

As the journey towards developing new insights into female serial killers encompassed the rich and complex areas of intersectionality and institutionalism, the authors had gleaned valuable insights that better assist an understanding of the dynamic relationship between Mary Ann and her institutional landscape. In the next chapter, questions of methodology are addressed.

DEVELOPMENT OF THE CASE STUDY

Introduction

Thus far, current challenges in the study of female serial killers have been outlined and intersectionality and institutionalism have been identified – key influences that would shape the approach to the study of Mary Ann's case. Within this chapter, the specific methodology deployed in the analysis of her case is described. The chapter will begin by explaining the process of arriving at a specific methodology before identifying the sources of data on which the authors drew. Following on from this, the framework through which the evidence was analysed will be presented and the limitations of the approach used will be considered.

The foundations of a method

In Chapter Two, the authors concurred with other criminologists in recognising the potential of institutionalism (Messner and Rosenfeld, 2004; Karstedt, 2010; Messner et al, 2013). While they wished to deviate somewhat from the positivist epistemology that characterise existing institutional studies of homicide, they did want to utilise some of the key concepts – notably 'institutional configurations' and 'social roles'. Developing a specific method would, however, be particularly challenging given the aims to both describe the institutional configurations of the Victorian society in which Mary Ann lived and explore how she engaged with the structural backdrop to her life. This was largely uncharted territory but the authors were not the first to be concerned about how to proceed. Indeed, the trailblazing criminologists who had played a central role in embedding institutional studies in criminology had noted: 'It is far easier to call for more and better institutional analysis in criminology than indicate precisely what such analysis should look like and how it ought to be implemented' (Messner and Rosenfeld, 2004, p 98). Such challenges were still very much present several years later when Richard Rosenfeld spoke on the subject to members of the American Society of Criminology in his presidential address:

> Just as we rightly tell macroresearchers their studies are not complete until they fill in the proximate causes of criminal behaviour, we also should encourage microresearchers to link the study of individuals to the big picture. But if we did, would they know how to do it? Would any of us? (Rosenfeld, 2011, p 2)

However, in reconsidering Messner and Rosenfeld's work, the authors began to develop a framework that held potential for addressing the epistemological imbalance. As noted in Chapter Two, Messner and Rosenfeld had identified three institutional dimensions – structure, regulation and performance (Messner and Rosenfeld, 2004; Messner et al, 2013). It is worth devoting some time to explaining them further here as these dimensions are central to the framework that was developed.

First, *institutional structure* – or the rules of the game to use Messner and Rosenfeld's terminology – refers to the systems of rules or norms that are the foundation of institutions. Such principles are, some argue, inherently socially constructed – constitutive of particular values or notions of morality, 'the humanly devised constraints that shape human interaction' (North, 1990, p 3). In relation to the economy, an example of such a rule might be engagement of men and women in paid labour as an appropriate way to support themselves. In terms of family rules we might include appropriate family structures for raising children. Structure also refers to the internal consistency of the rules or the extent to which they are mutually reinforcing within and across institutional domains. So, for example, while men and women's engagement in paid labour might be important in relation to participation in the economy, workers with dependent children may struggle to reconcile this with expectations placed on them in relation to their family lives and their status as 'good parents'.

Turning to examine *institutional regulation*, this is concerned with the extent to which people comply with the rules of the game and conform to the expectations placed on them as actors within these institutional domains. The sense of connection to other actors is an important factor in regulation:

> The distinctive feature of institutionalised social action is that it is governed by a sense of mutual obligation; actors align their behaviour with the rules of the game because they believe it is the right thing to do. Institutions therefore act as safeguards against purely opportunistic behaviour by encouraging attachments among individuals as well as commitment to the institution. (Rosenfeld and Messner, 2013, p 58)

A rule around good parenthood might be that women should withdraw from paid labour when they have a child and stay at home caring for that child until they are of school age. Regulation in relation to this rule is concerned with the degree to which mothers conform to it. Do they accept it as the right thing to do, fearing that defying it would result in them being labelled a 'bad mother', their family being seen as deficient and their child being 'let down'? Or do they defy this rule, perhaps because they are of the view that their participation in paid labour will enable their child to have a better quality of life or they feel an obligation to earn a wage because of a deep-seated work ethic and commitment to the economy? These are all examples of the 'moral force of the rules and the extrinsic sanctions and incentives that can be applied to influence behaviour' (Messner and Rosenfeld, 2004, p 93). As has been seen, compliance (or not) with the rules is inherently complex, particularly when the rules across institutional domains are contradictory rather than mutually reinforcing.

Finally, examining ideas of *institutional performance* involves assessing the extent to which compliance results in the rewards or outcomes expected in a particular institutional domain. So in terms of the economy and family examples used so far, does participating in paid labour result in financial independence and a good quality of life, and do mothers staying at home receive recognition as good mothers with well-adjusted children?

These institutional dimensions of structure, regulation and performance provided starting points from which to examine Mary Ann's case. In relation to each domain, the authors formulated several questions that they were interested in addressing. Regarding *structure*, questions focused on four areas:

- What institutions were central to/peripheral to/absent from the institutional context that Mary Ann inhabited?
- What was the nature of Mary Ann's social identity? Which social divisions were prominent/marginal? Furthermore, to what extent did elements of Mary Ann's social identity overlap or intersect to create her unique social identity?
- What were the rules of the game in relation to the institutional domains of relevance to Mary Ann? Were there internal or external inconsistencies within/between institutional domains?
- How should Mary Ann have been behaving in relation to the rules?

Turning to explore *regulation*, questions here were twofold:

- Primarily, to what extent did Mary Ann conform to the rules within each institutional domain?
- In addition, to what extent was the moral force of sanctions/incentives effective in constraining or enabling behaviour?

Finally, in relation to *performance*, the questions were as follows:

- Did adherence to or deviation from the rules result in the expected outcomes for Mary Ann?
- What was she achieving by the actions that she took? What outcomes were being secured?

In terms of how these questions would be answered, emphasis was placed on the social roles that Mary Ann occupied within and across the relevant institutional domains, for example wife, mother and income generator.

A case study

The authors decided that a case study approach would be most appropriate. This approach has been fruitfully deployed by previous scholars in studying female serial killers, flagging up themes and concepts that the broader quantitative surveys had not (Arrigo and Griffin, 2004; Myers et al, 2005; Frei et al, 2006; Orstroksy-Solis et al, 2008). The single case study held the greatest potential for generating deep and rich data. However, the authors wished to push the boundaries of existing research and go beyond a preoccupation with the individual's biography. The study of Mary Ann's case would additionally encompass the wider institutional configurations that formed the backdrop to her life and explore her relationship with these structures. This would be accomplished by an examination of her social roles in relation to structure, regulation and performance.

The authors' use of a single case study invites the criticism that one cannot generalise on this basis. However, such a criticism stems from the natural sciences, which test factors and variables, while here it is an outcome (albeit a highly dysfunctional and antisocial one) that is being explored – getting away with serial murder – and attempting to understand how this outcome came about. As such, this requires connectedness with the particulars of the case (Simons, 2009). Therefore, while the findings may not be formally generalised in the positivistic sense, they can contribute to the accumulation of knowledge relating to the micro–macro dynamics within institutionalist studies of serial murder, offering context-dependent insights and further highlighting the underestimated 'force of example' (Flyvbjerg, 2006, p 228). It can be argued that Mary Ann represents an extreme case study – intrinsically interesting because of its uniqueness (Yin, 2009) – but Flyvbjerg (2006, p 229) notes that such case studies 'often reveal more information because they activate more actors and more basic mechanisms in the situation studied'. Indeed, the case study approach was fundamental to some of the most influential criminologists of the 20th century – the Chicago School of the 1930s utilised the single case study extensively, with Shaw's (1930) *The jack-roller* being particularly poignant.

Data collection and analysis

The key sources of evidence in the case study were archival documents. The authors drew largely on local newspapers, which reported the trial in great detail, and examined records about Mary Ann held at the English National Archives, which were largely materials linked to her court appearances and prison life prior to her execution. However, in analysing this documentation, advice of case study proponents was heeded, notably that such evidence should not be taken as the unmitigated truth (Yin, 2009). As noted by Bosworth (2001, p 434), 'questions of evidence take on an entirely new aspect when interrogating the past'. Indeed, the evidence used represented embedded interpretations of reality and, as such, the authors sought to act as the 'vicarious observer' (Yin, 2009, p 105), seeking out the objectives that the documents' creators were attempting to meet and treating them as clues for further investigation rather than simply as findings in themselves. Consequently, local histories of north-east England were also incorporated (Bryant, 1942; Corfe, 1973; Thompson, 1976; Metcalfe, 2006), as were previous published works on Mary Ann Cotton (Appleton, 1973; Whitehead, 2000; Wilson, 2013) and local and regional newspapers, which reported local reaction to her crimes and reproduced personal correspondence, offering additional insights from Mary Ann herself and those friends and acquaintances who wrote to her while she was in prison.

It was particularly important given the emphasis on newspaper-based sources that the context within which these sources were located was acknowledged. The 19th century was a period in which the newspaper began to emerge as a valued and coveted source of information. Indeed, newspapers were the only form of media at this time (Wiener, 2007). Coverage of Mary Ann's case in the local press was more extensive than in the national press, which is not particularly surprising. After all, her trial took place in 1872, falling during the quarter century described by Walker (2006, p 382) as the 'heyday of the provincial newspaper'. Following the removal of a stamp duty in 1855, which had put newspapers out of the reach of many, provincial newspapers thrived. They progressed from being somewhat mild 'cut-and-pasted' versions of national newspapers to valuable mechanisms for the delivery of 'local news to a local readership … [and] papers were increasingly opinionated' (Walker, 2006, p 378). It has also been argued that 19th-century newspapers were written for and consumed by men, at least until the arrival of the 'new journalism' of the late 19th century, in which newspapers took on characteristics of more feminine mediums such as the magazine (Hampton, 2004a). Mary Ann's case arrived a few years prior to the new journalism, which enhanced the accessibility of newspapers to the working classes through changes in language and format, as well as price (Hampton, 2004b). Therefore, the main newspaper audience for Mary Ann's trial was largely male and middle class.

It is also important to consider at this point the representations of women accused of murder in the 19th century. Criminal trials were 'mass cultural spectacles' (Bland, 2008, p 626) where the 'boundaries of morality and normality were defined and redefined' (Bland, 2008, p 628). The timing of Mary Ann's trial is particularly important as press attention shone the spotlight on murder trials, particularly those in which the death sentence was a real possibility (Wiener, 2007). However, it has been claimed that there was a clear difference between local and national coverage of such cases, with the former elite and politically conservative papers being considerably more sympathetic to the accused than the latter popularly-aimed and more liberal papers (Tulloch, 2006; Wiener, 2007). Wiener (2007) goes on to consider the coverage of women accused of infanticide, and observes that local newspapers were often sympathetic in their portrayal of these women, sometimes leading petitions to have their death sentences commuted. However, an exception to this is noted:

> The last woman to be hanged in England for the murder of her own infant, Rebecca Smith in 1849, only went to the gallows because of the truly exceptional circumstances of her crime: she used the cold blooded method of arsenic poisoning, and after conviction she confessed to having similarly poisoned her seven other infants! In this case the press joined in a chorus of horror, the Globe calling her 'the annual and deliberate destroyer of her own offspring'. (Wiener, 2007, p 112)

There was general sympathy in cases where such actions were attributed to harsh social conditions in which the financial pressures created by another mouth to feed would plunge families further into poverty, but outright condemnation in cases that lay outside of this frame of reference. Pregnant women accused of murder were afforded some degree of protection by virtue of their status as expectant mothers. In 1848, one such woman – Charlotte Harris – was sentenced to hang for poisoning her husband in order to marry a wealthier, older gentleman. Following pressure from the press, which was instrumental in organising petitions, Harris's sentence was commuted (Wiener, 2007). Mary Ann did not secure such an outcome, despite attracting some sympathy from the public, which in effect only succeeded in postponing her execution until after she had given birth.

In summary, Mary Ann's case came at a pivotal time in the history of our modern mass media. It is perhaps fortunate that the case took place when provincial newspapers were at the height of their success as this fact has assisted in the reconstruction of the case. This aside, the literature suggests that those reporting on and reading about Mary Ann's trial came from a rather different, middle-class world to the one that she inhabited. Mindful of the above, the authors reviewed the source material independently of each other, using qualitative content analysis (Miles and Huberman, 1994; Coffey and Atkinson, 1996) to identify central concepts and themes. The analysis was organised in a table, with columns entitled social role, relevant institution(s) (polity, education, family, religion, economy), institutional dimension (structure, regulation, performance), key points and summary of/ quote from source material. The authors then discussed the findings, exploring points of both agreement and disagreement, and developed an interpretation of the unique ways in which Mary Ann worked and reworked her institutional templates (Hall and Taylor, 1996). Having explained the specific approach to the case study, findings are presented in the next chapter.

4
MARY ANN'S
SOCIAL ROLES

Introduction

The preceding chapters outlined the development of a new approach to understanding female serial killers, which would be used to analyse Mary Ann's case. This chapter will present the findings of the analysis, organised into subheadings relating to the social roles that Mary Ann occupied, exploring the institutional domain of these roles (economy, education, family, polity and religion) and the nature of her engagement with these configurations through the institutional dimensions of structure, regulation and performance. The chapter will draw heavily on source material, not only for explication purposes, but also to enable the reader to have a connectedness to the richness and complexity encountered when exploring the documentary evidence.

Wife

Marriage was essential for the survival of women in working-class, north-east England. Given Victorian legal and social frameworks, single women and widows were considerably less able to support themselves let alone any children they might have had (Wilson, 2013). But while women could cement a degree of security and respectability through marriage, they lived in the shadows, inferior and subordinate to the men in their lives (Metcalfe, 2006). In relation to the wives of coal miners, Hall (2004, p 522) acknowledges that their subordination was particularly pronounced: 'More than virtually all other working-class women, the vast majority of mining women were defined by, and defined themselves by, their home and family.' Furthermore, 'mining women were baby-makers and drudges, doubly oppressed by capitalism and by their husbands' (Hall, 2004, p 525). Indeed, women were often described in legal proceedings by their husband's occupation – as can be seen in the reporting of Mary Ann's own murder trial. The reverse was not true for male witnesses, who were identified by name and occupation:

> ... Isabella Smith, wife of Samuel Smith, living at South Hetton, fireman ... Sarah Smith, wife of William Smith, pitman, West Auckland ... Mary Ann Dodds, wife of Joseph Dodds ... Jonathan Townend, chemist, of West Auckland ... Mary Priestly, wife of John Priestly, pitman, of West Auckland ... Thomas Riley said: I am assistant overseer, grocer and draper, in West Auckland ... Richard William Barr said: I am one of the relieving officers of Bishop Auckland.... (*The Northern Echo*, 6 March 1873, pp 3-4)

The death of their spouse was one of the few conditions in which working-class wives could legitimately exit their marriage, as divorce was a particularly challenging and expensive undertaking (Fuchs and Thompson, 2005). In terms of the formation of her marriages, Mary Ann would appear to have been aware of the stigma of illegitimacy – respectable childbearing occurred only within wedlock (Smart, 1996; Carabine, 2001). She was always married (albeit bigamously in one instance) when she gave birth to her children but it was clear that the children had been conceived prior to the weddings. Referring to her marriage with her third husband, James Robinson, for example, *The Northern Echo* states: 'They were married secretly; at least, without the knowledge of Robinson's relations.... She gave satisfaction, and to avoid scandal he married her in 1867' (*The Northern Echo*, 25

March 1873, p 3). Remarriages were not uncommon in this area at the time – indeed, social historians have noted the commonality of single-parent and blended families in the 19th century given high adult and child death rates resulting from poverty and dangerous working conditions (Haines, 1977; Fuchs and Thompson, 2005). However, the number of times Mary Ann engaged in relationships and marriages was sufficient to draw critical comment from the *Newcastle Courant*: 'She surely must have had something particularly winning about her, seeing that she could with ease obtain one wooer and husband after another in rapid and exciting succession' (*Newcastle Courant*, 14 March 1873, p 5). Comments were also made regarding the paternity of the child to whom she gave birth in prison, which suggests that Mary Ann's sexual conduct had been noted and frowned upon by members of her community:

> Common report inclines to attribute the paternity to Nattrass, who lies in St. Helen's Churchyard. Other rumours point to men yet living in the neighbourhood who are supposed, not without reason, to have been "over kind", to use the old phrase, with Mrs Cotton, who, as we all know by this time, was by no means too strict in her notions of modesty. (*The Northern Echo*, 22 March 1873, p 3)

In other ways, Mary Ann appeared to adhere to structural templates. The nuclear families she created were well suited to the industrial age, enabling compact family units to move around as necessary (Parsons, 1959), prevalent among the mining communities in which Mary Ann lived (Hall, 2004). *The Northern Echo* reported that Mary Ann regularly moved around the country and the north-east region as dictated by her first husband's occupations:

> Mowbray belonged to Peterborough and frequently travelled about the country following the contractors by whom he was engaged. Shortly after marriage, the couple went south to Plymouth.... The date of her visit to Hetton was about 1856.

> Her husband was appointed foreman at the colliery.... A few
> years later they removed to Hendon, Sunderland. There Mr
> Mowbray, who had obtained employment as a stoker on the
> steam boat Mewburn, belonging to that port, established his
> home ... soon after the family removed [from Walbottle] to
> West Auckland, where the husband procured employment as a
> pitman in the West Auckland Colliery. (*The Northern Echo*, 25
> March 1873, p 3)

However, such mobility served another purpose – providing
opportunities to wipe the slate clean and to move away from channels
of regulation that might constrain her. The national press expressed
disbelief that her behaviour went undetected. *The London Standard*, for
example, commented: 'it seems surprising that such a woman could
live in towns and villages where everybody knows everybody else's
business without having been long ago brought to the justice by which
she has at length been overtaken' (*The London Standard*, 10 March 1873,
p 5). In addition, the same source emphasised the structural norm of
intra-social-class relationships, commenting on her interactions with
men both within and beyond these boundaries: 'The daughter of a
working collier, she had successfully set her cap at three men in her
own station of life, and she had also formed irregular connections with
other persons' (*The London Standard*, 10 March 1873, p 5). However,
these interpretations perhaps underestimated the extent to which
Mary Ann, described in *The Leeds Mercury* as a 'common-place, vulgar,
uneducated woman' (*The Leeds Mercury*, 8 March 1873, p 7) was able
to negotiate the institutional framework in such a way as to appear to
be conforming to the rules of the game. *The London Standard*'s view
also underestimated the heterogeneity of mining village life, which
was more characterised by 'comings and goings' than has previously
been thought (Wilson, 2013).

Wives managed the daily life of the household and being seen to have
a clean home was an important symbol of working-class respectability
(D'Cruze, 1995). Mary Ann appears to have been judged as a successful
wife in this regard, as witness testimony at her trial stated: 'Prisoner's

was a clean house' (*The Northern Echo*, 6 March 1873, p 3), and later comment reported: 'The prisoner was considered by many persons in the neighbourhood of West Auckland ... to be a clean and industrious woman' (*The Northern Echo*, 15 1873, p 3). This also enabled her access to soft soap and arsenic, which were part of a good house woman's toolkit but which she would use for altogether more sinister reasons (*The Northern Echo*, 8 March 1873). However, she deviated from the social norms to a degree by not cleaning the house herself, but paying other women to clean for her, which also involved sending them to purchase the soft soap and arsenic from local shops (*The Northern Echo*, 6 March 1873). The reporting of her trial identified several local women who provided this service. Her neighbour Mary Ann Dodds stated: 'I went there to clean ... I was employed to clean the house, and had been there often' (*The Northern Echo*, 6 March 1873, p 3). Another witness named Mary Tate gave similar testimony: 'I have been a great deal about her house cleaning' (*The Northern Echo*, 6 March 1873, p 3). Through this role as an employer, Mary Ann changed the balance of power in her relationships with these women from mutuality and reciprocity (Smith and Valenze, 1988) to dependency and subordination, limiting their capacity to act as a regulatory check on her behaviour.

Mother and stepmother

In terms of Mary Ann's role as a mother and a stepmother, several local norms of appropriate maternal behaviour became apparent. There was a general expectation that mothers would care for their children and stepchildren, as noted in the judge's summing up at Mary Ann's trial: 'You have been found guilty of murdering, by means of poison, your step son, whom you *ought* to have cherished and taken care of' (*The Northern Echo*, 8 March 1873, p 4, emphasis added). The disciplining of children through physical violence was, however, tolerated to an extent – witness Mr Davison stated in his testimony: 'These Durham lads want it some times' (*The Northern Echo*, 6 March 1873, p 3). However, other witnesses, including Mary Ann's neighbour Margaret

Priestley, suggested that she had taken disciplining her stepson Charles Edward Cotton a step too far:

> [S]he struck him against the wall with her hand. His head came against the wall. She took her foot up and bunched him … I could see that she often left him at eight o'clock in the morning, and didn't come back till late at night. She would lock him outside … I have five children, and I beat them in a right manner. I have what I call a belt in my house – it has no buckle on. I use it single. I never take my foot or knee to them.…The strap was one belonging to the lodger, with a buckle, such as pitmen wear. (*The Northern Echo*, 6 March 1873, p 3)

Furthermore, Mary Ann reportedly stated that Charles Edward was a burden and tried to get him admitted alone to the local workhouse – something that contravened legal codes around admittance to workhouses: '[I]t was not, according to the Poor Law, right to admit the child without the parent' (*The Northern Echo*, 8 March 1873, p 3). Therefore, such an attitude towards her stepson was considered deviant. Poor relief overseer Thomas Riley described this in his witness testimony: 'She said he [Charles Edward] was nothing to her … I see people when they apply for relief. It is rather rare that people complain of having to keep their husband's relations. I never remember such as case' (*The Northern Echo*, 6 March 1873, p 3). The words of relieving officer Richard William Barr were consistent with this view: 'I said I could not give such an order and she answered that the child was a great inconvenience to her. If it was not for the child, she could earn 10s. or 12s. per week.… She said it was not hers' (*The Northern Echo*, 6 March 1873, p 3). These contributions were reinforced by the testimony of police sergeant Thomas Hutchinson, whose words suggested that he saw Mary Ann as untrustworthy and that she may have been attempting to present herself as a victim:

> On the 12th July I received notice of the death of Charles Edward Cotton. On the 13th I told prisoner an inquest was

to take place. She said "Why?" I said because the doctors who had attended the boy during his illness had refused to grant a certificate for his burial. She said "Oh, people are saying that I poisoned him; but I am clear".... She said she had also wrote to an uncle of the boy's, to get him to take him, but he would not. She said she had had a good deal of trouble with Cotton's family – so many of them had died in so short a time. She said she was only his step mother, and had no right to keep him. She said "He has prevented me from earning many a pound". (*The Northern Echo*, 6 March 1873, p 4)

However, when considering her actions during Charles Edward's demise and after his death, other witnesses described socially acceptable behaviour from Mary Ann. For example, Archibald Chalmers – a doctor's assistant – stated in his witness testimony that Mary Ann 'showed every anxiety for the boy' (*The Northern Echo*, 6 March 1873, p 3). This was reinforced by her tears in court – her defence emphasised how she 'wept bitterly' when Charles Edward was being discussed (*The Northern Echo*, 8 March 1873, p 3). However, her behaviour was closely scrutinised by the prosecution:

[S]ome witnesses had admitted that prisoner was seen, during the illness of the child, to go with apparent anxiety for Dr Kilburn, and asked him to go and see the child....That was undoubtedly the conduct they would expect from an innocent person. Was it, or was it not, the conduct equally to be expected from a guilty person? If the prisoner had conceived the idea of taking away the life of the child, would she or would she not try to divert suspicion from herself and call in a medical man? (*The Northern Echo*, 8 March 1873, p 3)

A further point to note relating to the mother/stepmother role relates to burial insurance – policies for funeral expenses that paid out in the event of a family member's death (with a surplus often left over). The *Newcastle Courant* reported:

[T]he payment of even a small sum for every child that dies is often a premium on neglect, and those who have witnessed the levity with which the subject is discussed by the more ignorant and unfeeling women of the very lowest class will be inclined to suspect that it may be something more ... we could wish that life insurance among the very poor might assume some form which has the less appearance of offering inducements, if not to murder, at least to neglect. (*Newcastle Courant*, 14 March 1873, p 3)

Legislation in 1850 limited the amount that a child under the age of three could be insured for in order to tackle abuses (Rose, 1986). However, it could be argued that such interpretations represented the demonisation of poor people by the middle classes (Rowbotham, 1977), reinforced by prominent social commentators such as Spencer (1851) who emphasised their moral deficiencies. Burial insurance was commonplace in the area where Mary Ann resided, as confirmed in the witness testimony of James Young, a local agent for the Prudential Insurance Company at Mary Ann's trial. He stated: 'A vast number of the poorer classes insure in our office. It is a common thing for persons to insure a sum to bury the child decently with in case of death' (*The Northern Echo*, 6 March 1873, p 3). Mary Ann had indeed several times been the beneficiary of such payments following the deaths of members of her preceding families.

Worker

Working-class women's engagement in paid labour was common throughout England, as noted in the seminal work of Engels (1845). This was in distinct contrast to the experiences of middle-class women (Rose, 1992; Fuchs and Thompson, 2005) and was particularly prominent in the industrial north-east. However, paid work did not assign women any notable social status or prestige and their employment was often overlooked in official records – indeed, the section relating to occupation was left blank in Mary Ann's marriage certificate to her second husband George Ward, despite the fact that she was employed as a nurse at Sunderland Infirmary. In addition, average wages for single women in working-class communities were insufficient to maintain them above the poverty line so their relationship with the economy was strongly mediated by their gender role within the family (Wilson, 2013).

Relating to paid labour outside the home, Mary Ann had several jobs during her lifetime – as a nurse at Sunderland Infirmary, as a servant to a doctor and as a freelance nurse. Those who had worked alongside her at Sunderland Infirmary held her in high regard. This is clear in a letter to the Home Office from her former employer (Backhouse, 1873), who refused to accept her guilt and enclosed papers to urge a reprieve. *The Leeds Mercury* further reported on her time at Sunderland Infirmary:

> [W]hile there made a very favourable impression, by her general conduct, on those with whom she came into contact and those who employed her at and about that time.... The memorialists represent that the evidence of Mary Ann Cotton's guilt is entirely circumstantial. (*The Leeds Mercury*, 20 March 1873, p 8)

However, in her work as a servant, while she ensured that the work was completed and presented a favourable impression, she did not carry it out herself – subcontracting it to other women in much the same way she had done in relation to her own housework:

> At Spennymoor she remained for some months, and gained the reputation of being a business-like kind of a woman, who kept the house tidy enough, but by no means relished keeping it tidy herself. She preferred paying others to do it for her. (*The Northern Echo*, 25 March 1873, p 3)

Mary Ann also engaged in income-generating activities within the home. These roles included seamstress and landlady. She engaged in prostitution after the death of her second husband and following her break-up from her third husband:

> It is said on one hand that she obtained a living by taking in sewing work; on the other, that having no husband of her own, she contrived at once to gain a livelihood and supply the vacant place by receiving for payment as many men as cared to visit her. Whether as a seamstress or whether as a harlot, or whether – as is probable enough – as both, she continued living in widowhood until an advertisement attracted her notice... [after separating from James Robinson]. It is said vaguely that she had taken to the streets once more, and was to be found plying her vocation at Shields and Newcastle. (*The Northern Echo*, 25 March 1873, p 3)

The commentary that accompanied these observations by *The Northern Echo* was heavily gendered. The phrase 'having no husband of her own' implies that her behaviour, while deviant, was tolerated – she was no longer a married woman but a widow who was engaging in socially unacceptable behaviour only because she had no husband to provide for her. In relation to other work carried out at home, the discussion at her trial of her later role as a landlady highlighted additional points of relevance. The case for the defence drew on the testimony of two lodgers – brothers called George and William Taylor. The defence's interpretation of their testimonies suggest that the lodgers served a regulatory as well as a financial function – acting as a check on behaviour. The defence argued that Mary Ann could not have systematically poisoned Charles Edward without the lodgers noticing that something was amiss:

> [T]he Taylors had proved that they were lodging in the house at the time, and the meals of the Taylors were made ready by this woman. Did they suspect it? Did the jury believe that they would have lived as they did live with her for two months afterwards in the same cottage if they had suspected anything? She prepared their meals. She attended to them. She did all that

was necessary for them. Did they suspect it? (*The Northern Echo*, 8 March 1873, p 4)

However, another lodger by the name of William Lowrey did appear to have had his suspicions about Mary Ann. Lowrey visited and corresponded with Mary Ann while she was awaiting execution and wrote to *The Northern Echo* suggesting his thoughts as to her guilt:

> I got a letter from Mrs Cotton last week asking me to try and get up a petition to save her life. I sent word back that I thought there would be no chance for her and told her, in my simple way, to come to the cross of Christ, for He says, 'Let your sins be as red as scarlet, I will make them as white as snow. He that cometh unto me I will in no way cast out'. (Lowrey, 1873, p 119)

Acquisitive criminal

The murders Mary Ann committed were not her only criminal activities. During her marriage to James Robinson, she regularly stole from and defrauded him. Mary Ann appeared to have managed the Robinson household finances, something that was not unusual at the time (D'Cruze, 1995). However, she took advantage of this opportunity, as reported in *The Northern Echo*:

> After the death of the baby in Pallion, in December 1867, she seems to have stayed her hand from the slaughter. She did not, however, stay her fingers from her husband's pockets. Instead of paying his money into the building society, she spent it; she pawned articles of furniture and of clothes and involved her husband in debts to the amount of 60*l*. Robinson's eyes being opened at last, he remonstrated with her. He found that instead of having 21*l* in the Savings Bank, he had only 22*s*. (*The Northern Echo*, 25 March 1873, p 3)

Robinson had previously refused to permit Mary Ann to insure him or any of his children. It should also be noted that her marriage to Robinson was perhaps the most financially comfortable one – Robinson's occupation ensured that the family was wealthier than Mary Ann's other families. Indeed, Mary Ann did not need to steal from Robinson, and so it can be suggested that it wasn't the money itself but what stealing represented that was important – power over her husband. In her later letter to an old neighbour from her prison cell, she minimised her actions, saying simply: 'he and i not Egree We had sum Words Aboute sum money and i Left the house for a few days' (Cotton, 1873a, p 105). She went on to commit further fraudulent and other criminal activity when taking up employment as a servant for a doctor. The doctor was away and in his absence, Mary Ann subcontracted the work and funded this through criminal means:

> Her method of securing means to recompense these assistants was rather peculiar. She bought goods on credit, and gave them away as payment for services rendered. To one she would give a pair of stays, to another some article of wearing apparel; and in this manner the shopkeepers of Spennymoor were plundered to pay for her attendants. (*The Northern Echo*, 25 March 1873, p 3)

In the same way that no formal legal action came about from defrauding Robinson, so too was the case with the doctor: 'Missing some articles of value, he summoned her to his presence, and telling her of his suspicions, discharged her without calling in the police' (*The Northern Echo*, 25 March 1873, p 3). Mary Ann continued to engage in such behaviour in West Auckland – something that was to lay the foundation for her eventual apprehension. Thomas Riley had himself been a victim of Mary Ann's financial deviance, arguably causing him to be generally more cautious of her. It was reported: 'Mr Riley's son informed me that Mrs Cotton used to have an open account there, but having contracted debts to the extent of thirty shillings, he had stopped her credit, and after that everything she got she paid for' (*The Northern Echo*, 22 March 1873, p 3).

Murderer

The identity or label by which Mary Ann Cotton is now best known – a murderer – enables further insights into her positioning within the institutional backdrop. Prior to her conviction, Mary Ann performed the role of the innocent woman, but did so in such a way as to further raise suspicion. The witness testimony at her trial of the police sergeant Thomas Hutchinson – noted earlier – describes how she denied murder before she was even formally accused of such a crime (*The Northern Echo*, 8 March 1873). Following the inquest, which ruled that Charles Edward had been poisoned, *The Northern Echo* reported various exchanges between Mary Ann and her lodger Lowrey, in which she expressed a desire to flee and tried to sell him her furniture to raise the necessary funds: '[H]e endeavoured to dissuade her from her purpose, telling her how much such a course would strengthen the suspicions.... Subsequently she gave him to understand that it was her settled and determined intention to leave West Auckland' (*The Northern Echo*, 28 March 1873, p 3). Mary Ann had been trying to raise funds through other means, giving her cleaner items to pawn for her.

When convicted, Mary Ann's letters laid the blame for the guilty verdict at the hands of her rather ineffectual legal counsel and Thomas Riley, stating in a letter to childhood friend Henry Holdforth: 'I should not come to what i have for i had a first class Counsler to defend me' (Cotton, 1873b, p 106). In a letter to an unnamed old neighbour, she stated: 'i Am not guilty … Smith has Lead me rong if he told me not to speake A single Worde if i Was Asked Ever so hard or Ever so mutch…. As fore Riley god Will juge him, not A orthely judge' (Cotton, 1873a, p 105). Mary Ann also performed her innocence in exchanges with Mr and Mrs Edwards, neighbours who adopted the daughter she gave birth to in prison:

> "Good bye," said the convict; "and mind the bairn. And mind, when you take it over home with you to West Auckland, promise me that you'll never let Riley come near where it is – never, no never; and if it should be bad, you'll promise me that you'll

never have Dr Kilburn for to attend to it. Will you promise?"
(*The Northern Echo*, 22 March 1873, p 3)

Mary Ann never confessed to the murder of Charles Edward, despite
being urged to do so by both Lowrey and her stepfather George Stott.
His visit to her in prison prior to her execution suggests that he believed
she was guilty – of murdering both Charles Edward and her mother:

> Mr Stott informed her that he had delayed visiting her until
> this time, knowing that if she would confess she would confess
> to him. Mr Stott said, "Now, Mary Ann, thou hast not long to
> live now; and if thou hast anything to confess, do so now." She
> replied, "Father, I have not led a good life, but I am innocent of
> the crimes laid to my charge". (*The Northern Echo*, 24 1873, p 3)

Mary Ann also attempted to mobilise supporters in an attempt to secure
a reprieve, including her third husband James Robinson, but made it
clear that she held him partially responsible for her fate:

> ie must tell you Ar th Cause of All my trouble … you Know your
> sealfe i Am Knot guilty of the Lyies that has been told Consirning
> me … i hope you Will try to get my Life spared for ie Am not
> guilty of the crime ie have to dyie fore. (Cotton, 1873b, p 109)

She signed off letters to Robinson 'MAR' – an abbreviation of Mary
Ann Robinson. It could be argued that this was a way of trying to
convince him of the structural obligation towards her as his wife – they
had after all never formally divorced.

Mary Ann also evoked a further social role in order to rally support
for a reprieve – that of a Methodist Christian. In her correspondence
with Henry Holdforth (Cotton, 1873c), she used several references to
religion in trying to mobilise him – something not seen in her letters
to James Robinson, suggesting that she was using this man's religious
faith to better persuade him to assist her. This strategy was noted by
Matthew Hall – another childhood friend who wrote to Mary Ann,

fondly remembering the centrality of their Methodist faith in their formative years as children and teenagers. However, it appeared that Matthew Hall doubted the sincerity of Mary Ann's rediscovered faith:

> You seem to have a Hope of Heaven – be sure that Hope is well founded. A mere formal notion or wish, will avail you nothing, you must seek it earnestly with your whole heart, and with Tears – let not a moment slip … I write in the presence of God to take heed and let not your Soul be Lost through negligence or delay – but make immediate Effort and seek the Saviour. (Hall, 1873, p 124)

The only support for a reprieve came from Mary Ann's former colleagues at Sunderland Infirmary, as noted earlier – who had not seen her for several years – and those who had heard about her case in newspapers. Such appeals were apparently informed by structural templates for mothers – that they may be capable of murder if they were insane or experiencing extreme poverty (Arnot, 2000; McDonagh, 2003; Hager, 2008). One such example was a letter to the Home Secretary from a Dorchester woman, who stated: 'I dare say that in a state she thought the child would be better off than she could do for it … I do pray, humbly pray, that her life may be spared' (Olive, 1873, p 114). But the support from estranged colleagues and strangers was not matched by those in her own community: '[E]ven those who knew her as a friend and a neighbour should be so profoundly impressed with the magnitude of her crime, as to be unable even to sign a petition that her life may be spared' (*The Northern Echo*, 25 March 1873, p 3).

The reaction to Mary Ann's conviction sheds light on the structural institutional templates or rules of the game for women in north-east England in the 19th century and the extent to which Mary Ann apparently adhered to or deviated from the rules. The *Newcastle Daily Journal* stated: '[T]he most astounding thought of all is that a woman could act thus without becoming terrible and repulsive' (The West Auckland Poisonings, 1873, p 6). Journalists found it hard to make sense of Mary Ann as both a multiple murderer and a woman.

Her feminine appearance did not correlate well with her murderous activities at a time when the emergent work of Lombroso placed a heavy emphasis on the link between physical characteristics and criminal behaviour (Lombroso, 1875; Lombroso and Ferrero, 1885). Indeed, *The Northern Echo* included a short article reporting on a phrenological assessment of Mary Ann by Lowrey, perhaps seeking biological explanations for her deviance:

> Mr Lowrey, who is an amateur phrenologist, has supplied us with the following, derived from a cursory examination of the prisoner's head in the condemned cell: - Veneration small; no love for children; destructiveness very large ; secretiveness very large ; calculation good ; language deficient. (*The Northern Echo*, 28 March 1873, p 3)

Such sense making was also reflected in how Mary Ann's physical appearance was portrayed – it is claimed that newspaper pictures of her were deliberately coarsened to make her appear more frightening (Appleton, 1973), clearly more in keeping with notions of what a murderer would look like.

Throughout this chapter, we have explored the social roles that Mary Ann occupied during her life, the institutional domain of these roles (economy, education, family, polity and religion) and the nature of her interaction with these structures through the institutional dimensions of structure, regulation and performance. Key findings in terms of these relationships are summarised in Table 4.1. Their implications are considered in the next chapter.

4. MARY ANN'S SOCIAL ROLES

Table 4.1: Summary of findings

Social role	Institutional domain(s)	Structure	Regulation	Performance
			Institutional dimension	
Wife	Economy Family Polity Religion	Marriage/ widowhood/ remarriage Dependency Husband's work Respectable women Clean home	Excessive and rapid remarriages Exceeded what was 'normal' Geographical mobility Respectable veneer Cleaners	Obtained expected outcomes Destroyed multiple manifestations of the family
Mother	Family	Cherish and care for children Parental responsibility, prioritisation of children's needs Acceptable discipline Acceptable infanticide	Performed role of good mother Own needs first Overstepped discipline boundaries Unacceptable murder	Failed to obtain expected outcomes Excessive child mortality
Worker	Economy Family	Working-class women and paid labour Little recognition Supplement husband's income Home workers – landlady, seamstress, prostitute	Nurse Servant Children – barrier to paid labour for a widow Landlady	Generated income from paid labour Income from lodgers Surveillance of lodgers – damage limitation
Christian	Polity Religion	Wesleyan Methodist Church Responsibility through confession Repentance	Part-time Wesleyan Never confesses, blames others for acquisitive crimes Religion as a protective mechanism	Re-engagement with religion fails to secure reprieve Matthew Hall questions her sincerity
Fraudster Thief	Economy Family	Acquisitive crime – capitalism Victims – extra familial Getting caught – consequences	No material **need** to commit acquisitive crime Victims – familial and employer Getting away with it	Acquisitive crime for power, not greed Defrauding rather than depending on men
Murderer	Family Polity	Tolerance of infanticide Women who kill – mad / bad / insane / evil Burial insurance	Not infanticide, many children older than 12 months Systematic planned murders Social construction of a monster Husbands and children insured	Insurance Murder as emancipation?

AN INSTITUTIONAL UNDERSTANDING OF MARY ANN AND FUTURE DIRECTIONS FOR RESEARCH

Introduction

This chapter draws together the findings from the analysis and considers how the approach taken was useful in making sense of Mary Ann in ways that existing frameworks for understanding female serial killers are not. The authors will argue that this approach – termed *institutional mediation* – has the potential to be a trailblazer for broader understandings of individual female serial killers. In addition, the chapter also considers future directions for the use of institutional mediation beyond serial homicide.

Towards a new understanding of female serial killers

The authors set out with the aim of generating insights into how Mary Ann was able to get away with murder for as long as she did. Such a study was far from simple as it would involve both a more robust analysis of the social and cultural context of an individual serial killer and an appreciation of the gendered nature of the relevant structures. These elements had been somewhat neglected in the quantitative surveys, typologies and individual case studies on which existing insights into female serial killers have been built in the past. The literature around female serial killers is characteristic of the epistemological imbalance described by Messner (2012) in that macro quantitative surveys and typologies do not consider micro implications, and individual case studies at the micro level are preoccupied with such detail at the expense of the broader macro context.

Having considered the institutional literature, sociological institutionalism was identified as particularly valuable, emphasising a dynamic relationship between individuals and institutions and a central role for cultural components such as values, beliefs and norms (Meyer and Rowan, 1977; Brinton and Nee, 1998; Peters, 1999). Sociological institutionalists have argued that individuals actively work and rework institutional scripts to devise a course of action mindful of mainstream norms and values (March and Olsen, 1989, 1998; Powell and DiMaggio, 1991; Fligstein, 1997; Brinton and Nee, 1998). While the authors wished to diverge from the positivist epistemology that characterises institutional studies of homicide, they identified key concepts from the institutional literature that they wanted to explore – notably 'social roles' and 'institutional configurations'. In addition, the intersectional literature's emphasis on individual *experiences* of structurally embedded social divisions was noted, something that institutional theorists have also acknowledged as important – particularly in relation to gender (Potter, 2006; Bernard, 2013; Applin and Messner, 2015). Documentary sources in relation to Mary Ann's case were then analysed to explore both institutional configurations of the society in which she lived and her lived experience of these structural arrangements through social roles and identities. In the next section, key findings and their implications for criminological insights into her case are outlined.

An institutionally embedded serial killer

Considering institutional performance in relation to her social roles, first as a wife, Mary Ann did achieve the expected outcomes of respectability and a degree of financial security. However, the frequency with which she remarried was out of the ordinary and her sexual conduct as a widow was deemed inappropriate when viewed through the structural rules of the game that set boundaries for the behaviour of wives. Hiring other women to do her cleaning for her was also unusual for a working-class woman but served to alter the power balance in her relationships with her female contemporaries – she positioned herself not as their equal (Smith and Valenze, 1988) but as their employer, someone on whom they were dependent. As such, this had a detrimental impact on the extent to which other women were able to act as the regulators of her behaviour. In being someone on whom other women depended for income, Mary Ann weakened her attachments with them, in so doing also diluting the sense of mutual obligation that underpinned this regulation (Rosenfeld and Messner, 2013).

Turning to examine her role as a mother, given the high rates of infant mortality and ill-health that were prevalent in north-east England in the 19th century, the social conditions were such that *some* of Mary Ann's children might not have been expected to reach adulthood. However, this was the fate that befell *most* of her children. Rather than nurturing and caring for them – central rules of the game within the family – Mary Ann seemed intent on pursuing her own ends, seeing her children as an inconvenience. The murders of her children and stepchildren were not the altruistic actions of an insane (Arnot, 2000) or impoverished mother saving her children from miserable lives (McDonagh, 2003; Hager, 2008) but a woman disposing of children who had compelled her into marriage and were the unfortunate side effect of performance of the wife social role.

As a worker, Mary Ann was able to bring additional money into the home when she was married – consistent with the rules of the game for working-class women (Engels, 1845; Rose, 1992; Fuchs and

Thompson, 2005). However, she also seemed to survive when she was widowed – taking in lodgers was particularly fruitful. Essentially, Mary Ann was able to subsist in a social context where this was very difficult for a woman in her position (Wilson, 2013). She was to a degree deviating from the rules of the game in being a self-sufficient single woman achieving financial security on her own. While a degree of financial security was an expected outcome in Victorian society, it was one that was more commonly achieved by men as the main breadwinners and heads of household. Taking in lodgers did, however, bring about attachments with individuals who were a potential source of regulation (Rosenfeld and Messner, 2013), introducing a new channel of surveillance as well as an income for Mary Ann. Lowrey's words did nothing to persuade others of her innocence and suggested that as a member of her household he may have at least suspected Mary Ann of failing to align her behaviour with the rules of the game. However, the fact that the surveillance of lodgers did not directly uncover her crimes and lead to her apprehension suggests that the lodgers were unable to anticipate that Mary Ann could be a murderer, so at odds was this with her feminised social roles and identities.

By virtue of her sociodemographic and physical characteristics, Mary Ann did not make sense within the structural templates of criminal women of the 19th century and, as such, was able to continue her acquisitive and murderous criminal activities unchecked for a considerable period of time. Her acquisitive crime in particular could not be explained by greed or an appetite for consumer goods. It could be argued that these crimes were about power – by stealing money from her husband and defrauding her employer, she was gaining control over men. As noted earlier, institutional structure dictated that women were dependent on and inferior to men in north-east England in the 19th century (Hall, 2004; Metcalfe, 2006). In stealing from them, Mary Ann was turning this upside down. Her murders were understood by Victorian England as financially motivated and therefore wholly explained by the burial insurance policies she was able to cash in on when her relatives died. If this is true then she succeeded for a while, achieving the expected economic outcomes. However, these were relatively small sums of money, she could by no means retire on them and indeed she had proved herself to be quite versatile and successful at supporting herself financially when she needed to.

It is therefore argued that Mary Ann's choices to systematically create and destroy multiple manifestations of the family could be interpreted as more or less emancipatory efforts – albeit dysfunctional and antisocial ones – to break gender norms and perform a homicidal protest (Wilson, 2007) against the one institution that constrained her but provided the only institutional location in which she could obtain respectable womanhood – the family. The authors argue that Mary Ann was performing gender (West and Zimmerman, 1987) against an institutional backdrop within which her potential courses of action were confined to the family through the social roles of the wife and the mother. Roles and identities incompatible with the wife and the mother – most notably the murderer – simply went unseen. As such, the gender power imbalance of 19th-century Victorian England enabled Mary Ann to get away with murder for many years. She was able to work and rework the institutional scripts (March and Olsen, 1989, 1998; Powell and DiMaggio, 1991; Fligstein, 1997; Brinton and Nee, 1998) until she began to present an inconsistent performance to her audiences in West Auckland. Notable within these audiences was Thomas Riley. In his position as grocer, draper and overseer of poor relief, he had a greater number of attachments to the individuals in his locality and, as such, a larger volume of information about them than was the case for other villagers. In this unique position he was an important agent of institutional regulation (Rosenfeld and Messner, 2013).

Institutional anomie theory (IAT) posits that the dominance of the economy is harmful in contemporary society, as economic roles are prioritised over non-economic roles such as those relating to the family and religion (Messner and Rosenfeld, 2007). It is argued that such arrangements make particular types of acquisitive and violent criminal behaviour more likely as individuals strive for economic outcomes and experience the effects of economic dominance. Mary Ann's case is not one of institutional dominance or institutional anomie but institutional *constraint*. Here the authors are referring to the degree of flexibility or institutional elasticity that existed around the rules of the game. In the case of Mary Ann, there was a very low degree of institutional elasticity – the rules for working-class women were rigid and prescriptive. As such, they constrained her choices or scripts, but also acted to ensure that others would never conceive of her as a serial killer as this did not fit with the rules of the game for women in their traditional social roles.

The analysis in this book diverged from the epistemological positivism that has characterised other institutional endeavours in criminology – it transcended structural configurations at a societal level to examine individual institutional experience. A number of previous institutional studies of homicide have focused on women's risk of victimisation within particular institutional arrangements, arguing that as they move out of traditional gender roles they are exposed to greater risks (Gartner et al, 1990; Stamatel, 2014). Other studies have identified a positive association between female-perpetrated homicide and institutional arrangements that tend to increase women's marginalisation (Pridemore, 2007; Gruenewald and Pridemore, 2009) – creating conditions in which 'sheer desperation' (Brookman, 2005, p 181) can thrive. These studies emphasise the status of women as victims, even as the perpetrators of homicide, a common method of sense making around women who kill (D'Cruze et al, 2006). However, in Mary Ann, we are dealing not with a woman who was a victim in this way but an aggressor who rejected the legitimacy of the family as the only social institution in which women could exist as members of society. Mary Ann failed to accept the moral validity of the family (LaFree, 1998). She also rejected the legitimacy of the state's monopoly on legitimate force and homicide, taking decisions of life and death into her own hands, highlighting the potential relevance of macro literature claiming an inverse relationship between state legitimacy and homicide (Nivette and Eisner, 2013). Rather than examining risks of women becoming victims of homicide in the move away from traditional social roles, the authors found instead a woman who had become a serial perpetrator of homicide while constrained in traditional social roles.

Mary Ann experienced a dynamic relationship with the institutions that formed the backdrop to her life – she successfully performed socially acceptable behaviour within them by drawing on mainstream norms and values. She was able to get away with murder because the gendered institutional configurations not only dictated her constrained social position but also ensured that no one would suspect a woman of such heinous crimes. It was not so much that institutional regulation in Victorian society was ineffective but that the rules of the game on which regulation drew did not expect this level of extreme deviance and, as such, was unable to recognise it soon enough to prevent further murders.

Institutional mediation beyond Mary Ann

Having examined the available evidence in the case of the Mary Ann Cotton, it can be argued that the approach adopted – *institutional mediation* – has the potential to generate richer insights into serial killing. The term 'institutional mediation' is used to describe it because the approach enables a consideration of the mediating role of institutions in terms of the nature and extent of influence on individual choices and actions. Such insights can transcend those offered by quantitative surveys, typology and case studies that dominate current theorising around female serial killers. Institutional mediation enables serial killers to be located within a wider framework that accommodates social and cultural factors, considering the ways in which structure and agency come together to create opportunity.

With reference to Britain, a small number of scholars – one of the authors included – have previously suggested that the social and cultural context is an important missing piece in the jigsaw puzzle of understanding serial murder (Soothill, 2001; Soothill and Wilson, 2005; Wilson, 2009):

> [T]he responsibility for serial killing does not lie so much with the individual serial killer, but can be better found within the social and economic structure of Britain since the 1960s, which

> ... does not reward the efforts of all and in particular marginalised large sections of society.... (Wilson, 2007, p 17)

It is notable that the high-point of British serial killing was in 1986 – when four serial killers were active, a period that also coincided with the high-point of Thatcherism (Wilson, 2009). Thatcherism did not simply describe the administrative period of Prime Minister Margaret Thatcher but also the economic and political ideology advocated by her government, which was distinctly neoliberal (Harvey, 2005). Such a philosophy prioritised a rolling back of the state towards a minimalist welfare safety net and a commitment to monetarist economic policy, the antithesis of the interventionism that characterised Keynesian economic management. This represented a considerable move away from the social democratic consensus of the post-war governments – the emphasis was no longer on social equality and a comprehensive welfare state but on freedom of the market and the self-reliance of individual citizens (Timmins, 1995). The late 20th century was a period associated with widening social and economic inequality, where the gap between the richest and poorest segments of society grew considerably (Jordan, 1998; Wilkinson and Pickett, 2010). The Conservative Party was described as 'an uncaring Party that is indifferent to the plight of those in poverty and hostile towards groups such as single mothers who are deemed to pose a threat to the family and traditional social values' (Page, 2010: 147). It is perhaps no coincidence that victims of serial murder were the very individuals whose lifestyles and values ran counter to the institutional structures and rules of the game advocated by those occupying key roles in the polity and those who were being increasingly marginalised in such institutional configurations – including prostitutes, older people, young runaways and gay men. The authors argued in a recent paper:

> [S]erial killers exploit fractured communities, in which some lives are seen as more valuable than others and where increasingly people have to struggle simply to survive. So in this dreadful way serial killing tells us something about our culture, our values and

our civic society. It emerges as the elephant in the sitting room of public policies that create a culture of "them" and "us" and a society where there is a widening gap between the "haves" and the "have nots". In such societies it is presumed that some people simply do not have value for the development of that society, and can therefore be cast adrift as challenging the status quo and unrepresentative, or as a burden on the state's resources. (Wilson and Yardley, 2013, p 27)

Having since developed the concept of 'institutional mediation', the authors believe that a more detailed examination of individual cases using this approach would enable us to go further in our analysis, considering not only the institutional arrangements – which appear to be the very embodiment of IAT in this example – but also the extent to which agency, through intersecting social identities and roles, combine with those institutional configurations to create opportunity for serial murder. This may also help to generate new insights into why some serial killers operated undetected for decades while others were caught relatively quickly.

While it is not within the scope of this book to analyse additional cases in the same depth as Mary Ann's, it is certainly worth exploring how institutional mediation might be deployed to shed light on other examples. Doctor Harold Shipman murdered an estimated 215 people between 1975 and 1998. Nurse Beverly Allitt killed four children and attempted to kill nine others between February and April of 1991. Drawing on institutional mediation, the authors would examine the rules of the game for Shipman and Allitt in their professional roles as well as other roles such as father, husband, colleague, daughter and student. They would explore how their performances in these roles were affected by intersections of age, gender, class and other social divisions. They would look at whether institutional structure was sufficiently malleable to encompass the idea that someone occupying such an institutional location could commit serial murder. The authors hypothesise that Shipman, as a male, middle-aged doctor in a society in which the authority of such individuals is rarely questioned, was institutionally better positioned to get away with murder than a young, inexperienced and somewhat immature Beverly Allitt. So while the institutional structures were sufficiently flexible and ready to conceive of Allitt as a serial killer, the same could not be said in relation to Shipman.

The authors believe that institutional mediation could also be fruitfully deployed in understandings of murder beyond serial killing. Exploring the nature of institutional structure and the degree of regulation around the rules of the game does appear to hold potential for understanding how some murders are able to happen despite clear breaches of the institutional rules of the game having occurred in the preceding period. The case referred to here is that of Daniel Pelka. This is a case with which the authors are particularly familiar as it happened in the Midlands region of England, where they live and work – the authors closely followed the case, and commented on it in local and national media, having reviewed documentary evidence in the public domain. Four-year-old Daniel was systematically starved and beaten by his mother Magdalena Łuczak and his stepfather Mariusz Krężołek for several months before his death in March 2012. Both parents were found guilty of his murder and each sentenced to a minimum of 30 years' imprisonment. In relation to institutional structure, Daniel's mother and stepfather were clearly not abiding by the rules of the game in relation to the family in contemporary society, which dictate that young children are vulnerable and in need of adults' love and care (Aries, 1962; Goldstein et al, 1984; Corsaro, 1997). Unlike the institutional structure that formed the backdrop of Mary Ann's childrearing, violence against children is now very clearly prohibited by law. Łuczak prioritised her role as Krężołek's partner over that of her role as Daniel's mother and the couple lived a chaotic existence, their household characterised by domestic abuse and alcohol misuse:

> [Y]our relationship has been revealed on the evidence to be an intense and stormy one, marked by heavy drinking, mutual acts of aggression and yet strong physical attraction.... Both of you are in breach of what is probably the most important position

of trust, as the parents of a small child who was entitled to their protection, their love and their care. Your breach of trust Magdalena Łuczak, is wholly irreconcilable with the loving care that a mother should show towards her own son.... (*R v Mariusz Krężołek and Magdalena Łuczak*, 2013, pp 5-6)

What appeared to puzzle observers of this case was not so much the fact that Łuczak and Krężołek were capable of such cruelty but the fact that professionals appeared to have 'failed' in their duty to safeguard Daniel's wellbeing. This case is not solely about individuals breaking the structural rules, but additionally encompasses the perceived failure of institutional regulation to detect such rule breaking and prevent Daniel's death. Blame was laid at the hands of schoolteachers, health visitors, police officers and social workers, all of whom had had contact with the family. Unlike Thomas Riley, the grocer, draper and overseer of poor relief in West Auckland whose diverse range of roles enabled him to have a broad overview of Mary Ann's family life and confidence on which to base his suspicions, the professionals who saw into Daniel's family life did so largely in exclusion from each other and were not able to take in the bigger picture:

> Ms Łuczak's assertions that circumstances had changed and improved were taken without sufficient challenge and her alcohol misuse was not fully addressed.... In summary therefore most incidents were dealt with in isolation and the cumulative effect of domestic abuse was not sufficiently recognised by any of the involved agencies. (Coventry Local Safeguarding Children's Board, 2013, p 41)

From an initial consideration of the evidence available, it can be suggested that understanding this case benefits from institutional mediation. Like the other cases discussed, there is a clear lack of institutional flexibility. However, this extends beyond structure to also encompass regulation. In contemporary society, the regulation of the rules of the game sits within the formal as opposed to the informal sphere when it comes to the family. 'Safeguarding' children is now seen as an occupational task for human services personnel rather than a mutual obligation among members of society. State actors working in this capacity are tasked with enforcement rather than support, particularly given the increasing bureaucratisation of social work (Howe, 1992; Harris, 2003). This is particularly true in the age of austerity. Lower-level preventative services tasked with identifying early warning signs and putting support in place to prevent the escalation of problems have been cut back and resources targeted at cases with higher levels of need. In essence, this means that by the time families with problems come onto the radar of professionals their needs are often urgent and acute. These processes are supported by the concept of 'privacy' – a relatively new rule of the game in relation to the family – which is strongly associated with the neoliberal philosophy of late 20th-century Western governments. Other people's family lives are increasingly conceptualised as no one else's business. 'Privacy' is held up as a valuable neoliberal concept – it enables people to have control over who has information about their families and who has access to their family spaces and places (McKie, 2005). However, privacy acts as the barrier behind which the suffering of Daniel Pelka and others like him can thrive and it also acts as a legitimate reason for actors within informal social networks *not* to act on their suspicions or intervene when they are concerned about a child – effectively *denying* the existence of abuse and neglect (Cohen, 2013). In cases such as that of Daniel Pelka, the institutional rules of the game in relation to the family have become increasingly complex and internally inconsistent. While the institutional structure of the family could be described as more child centred than that of the Victorian era, the new rule of privacy now screens the dark side of the family from public view. Compounding this is the professionalisation – and to some extent privatisation (Rogowski, 2012) – of regulation around this institution, effectively removing mutual obligation within informal networks to monitor the behaviour of others in adhering to the rules of the game and putting the emphasis on the business of safeguarding and those charged with this task – social workers, police officers, health visitors and schoolteachers.

If there are any preventative lessons to be learned from institutional mediation in relation to these cases, one thing appears to be very clear. What is common across all of the cases discussed in this chapter is a need for increased institutional elasticity – both in terms of who we consider capable of killing others and in terms of who we hold responsible for regulating behaviour to prevent such murders from occurring. Too often our conceptualisation of what a murderer *looks like* are shaped by the tendency of the existing literature to categorise and identify typical offenders. We often make sense of their crimes using simplified and media-friendly stock narratives of mad, bad or evil people (D'Cruze et al, 2006). However, as we have seen, female serial killers and, the authors would argue, other perpetrators of homicide, are a complex combination of social roles and identities embedded within particular institutional configurations. As such, understandings of homicide and preventative efforts can only benefit from institutional mediation in its consideration of how agency and structure come together to create the opportunity for murder.

In developing the concept of 'institutional mediation', the authors believe that they have demonstrated an innovative – albeit exploratory – approach that helps to close the epistemological gap in relation to understanding female serial killing and beyond. Examples of how this concept might be applied have been provided and it will now be necessary to analyse a wider range of cases to develop the concept further. Given its strength as an interdisciplinary field, 21st-century criminology is in a strong position to take on this task.

REFERENCES

Adjorlolo, S and Chan, HC, 2014, The controversy of defining serial murder: revisited, *Aggression and Violent Behaviour*, 19, 5, 486-491

Appleton, A, 1973, *Mary Ann Cotton: Her story and trial*, London: Michael Joseph

Applin, S and Messner, SF, 2015, Her American dream: bringing gender into institutional anomie theory, *Feminist Criminology*, 10, 1, 36-59

Aries, P, 1962, *Centuries of childhood: A social history of family life*, New York, NY: Vintage

Arnot, M, 2000, Understanding women committing new-born child murder in Victorian England, in S D'Cruze (ed) *Everyday violence in Britain 1850-1950*, Harlow: Longman, 55-69

Arrigo, BA and Griffin, A, 2004, Serial murder and the case of Aileen Wuornos: Attachment theory, psychopathy, and predatory aggression, *Behavioral Sciences & the Law*, 22, 3, 375-393

Backhouse, E, 1873, Letter to William Tallack, Home Office, March 20, in A Appleton, *Mary Ann Cotton: Her story and trial*, London: Michael Joseph, 114-115

Bartol, CR and Bartol, AM, 2004, *Introduction to forensic psychology*, London: Sage Publications

Bernard, A, 2013, The intersectional alternative: explaining female criminality, *Feminist Criminology*, 8, 1, 3-19

Bland, L, 2008, The trials and tribulations of Edith Thompson, *Journal of British Studies*, 47, 3, 624-648

Bonn, S, 2014, *Why we love serial killers: The curious appeal of the world's most savage murderers*, New York, NY: Skyhorse Publishing

Bosworth, M, 2001, The past as a foreign country: some methodological implications of doing historical criminology, *British Journal of Criminology*, 41, 3, 431–442

Bouchier, D 1983, *The feminist challenge*, London: Macmillan

Brinton, MC and Nee, V, 1998, *The new institutionalism in sociology*, Stanford, CA: Stanford University Press

Britton, DM, 2000, Feminism in criminology: engendering the outlaw, *The Annals of the American Academy of Political and Social Science*, 571, 1, 57–76

Brookman, F, 2005, *Understanding homicide*, London: Sage Publications

Bryant, A, 1942, *English saga 1840-1940*, London: The Reprint Society

Burgess-Proctor, A, 2006, Intersections of race, class, gender and crime: future directions for feminist criminology, *Feminist Criminology*, 1, 1, 27–47

Burrell, G and Morgan, G, 1979, *Sociological paradigms and organisational analysis*, London: Heinemann

Carabine, J, 2001, Unmarried motherhood 1830-1990: a genealogical analysis, in M Wetherell, S Taylor and SJ, Yates (eds) *Discourse as data: A guide for analysis*, London: Sage Publications, 267–310

Carlen, P, 1983, *Women's imprisonment*, London: Routledge & Kegan Paul

Carlen, P, 1985, *Criminal women*, Oxford: Polity Press

Carlen, P, 1988, *Women, crime and poverty*, Milton Keynes: Open University Press

Carlen, P and Worrall, A (eds), 1987, *Gender, crime and justice*, Milton Keynes: Open University Press

Cavadino, M and Dignan, J, 2006, *Penal systems: A comparative approach*, London: Sage Publications

Chan, W, 2001, *Women, murder and justice*, Basingstoke: Palgrave Macmillan

Chesney-Lind, M, 2006, Patriarchy, crime and justice: feminist criminology in an era of backlash, *Feminist Criminology*, 1, 1, 6–26

Coffey, A and Atkinson, P, 1996, *Making sense of qualitative data: Complementary research strategies*, Thousand Oaks, CA: Sage Publications

REFERENCES

Cohen, S, 2013, *States of denial: Knowing about atrocities and suffering* (2nd edn), Oxford: Wiley

Corfe, T, 1973, *Sunderland: A short history*, Newcastle: Frank Graham

Corsaro, WA, 1997, *The sociology of childhood*, Thousand Oaks, CA: Sage Publications

Cotton, MA, 1873a, Letter to an unnamed old neighbour, March 11, in A Appleton, *Mary Ann Cotton: Her story and trial*, London: Michael Joseph, 105

Cotton, MA, 1873b, Letter to Henry James Robinson, March 12, in A Appleton, *Mary Ann Cotton: Her story and trial*, London: Michael Joseph, 109

Cotton, MA, 1873c, Letter to Henry Holdforth, March 11, in A Appleton, *Mary Ann Cotton: Her story and trial*, London: Michael Joseph, 106-07

Coventry Local Safeguarding Children's Board, 2013, *Serious case review: Overview report: Daniel Pelka*, Coventry: Coventry Coventry Local Safeguarding Children's Board

D'Cruze, S, 1995, Women and the family, in J Purvis (ed) *Women's history: Britain 1850-1945*, London: Routledge, 51-84

D'Cruze, S, Walklate, S and Pegg, S, 2006, *Murder*, London: Routledge

D'Orban, PT, 1990, Female homicide, *Irish Journal of Psychological Medicine*, 7, 1, 64-70

Daly, K and Stephens, DJ, 1995, The 'dark figure' of criminology: towards a black and multi-ethnic feminist agenda for theory and research, in N Hahn Rafter and F Heidensohn (eds) *International feminist perspectives in criminology: Engendering a discipline*, Philadelphia, PA: Open University Press, 189-215

Dietz, P, 1986, Mass, serial and sensational homicide, *Bulletin of the New York Academy of Medicine*, 62, 5, 477-91

Douglas, JE, Burgess, AW, Burgess, AG and Ressler, RK, 1992, *Crime classification manual: A standard system for investigating and classifying violent crime*, New York, NY: Simon & Schuster

Egger, S, 1984, A working definition of serial murder and the reduction of linkage blindness, *Journal of Police Science and Administration*, 12, 3, 348-357

Egger, S, 1998, *The killers among us: An examination of serial murder and its investigation*, Upper Saddle River, NJ: Prentice Hall

Engels, F, 1845, *The condition of the working class in England*, London: Penguin, 1987

Farrell, AL, Keppel, RD and Titterington, VB, 2011, Lethal ladies: revisiting what we know about female serial murderers, *Homicide Studies*, 15, 3, 228-252

Farrell, AL, Keppel, RD and Titterington, VB, 2013, Testing existing classifications of serial murder considering gender: an exploratory analysis of solo female serial murderers, *Journal of Investigative Psychology and Offender Profiling*, ahead of print, doi: 10.1002/jip.1392

FBI (Federal Bureau of Investigation), 2008, *Serial murder: Multidisciplinary perspectives for investigators*, Washington, DC: Behavioral Analysis Unit, National Center for the Analysis of Violent Crime, U.S. Department of Justice

Ferguson, CJ, White, DE, Cherry, S, Lorenz, M, and Bhimani, Z, 2003, Defining and classifying serial murder in the context of perpetrator motivation, *Journal of Criminal Justice*, 31, 3, 287-292

Ferrell, J, 2005, Crime and culture, in C Hale, K Hayward, A Wahidin and E Wincup (eds) *Criminology*, Oxford: Oxford University Press, 139-15

Fligstein, N, 1997, Social skill and institutional theory, *American Behavioural Scientist*, 40, 4, 397-405

Flyvbjerg, B, 2006, Five misunderstandings about case-study research, *Qualitative Inquiry*, 12, 2, 219-245

Franklin, DB, 2006, *The good-bye door: The incredible true story of America's first female serial killer to die in the chair*, Kent, OH: Kent State University Press

Frei, A, Völlm, B, Graf, M and Dittmann, V, 2006, Female serial killing: review and case report, *Criminal Behaviour and Mental Health*, 16, 3, 167-176

Fuchs, RG and Thompson, VE, 2005, *Women in nineteenth-century Europe*, Basingstoke: Palgrave Macmillan

REFERENCES

Garland, D, 1985, *Punishment and welfare: A history of penal strategies*, Aldershot: Gower

Garland, D, 2001, *The culture of control*, Oxford: Oxford University Press

Gartner, R, 1991, Family structure, welfare spending, and child homicide in developed democracies, *Journal of Marriage and the Family*, 53, 1, 231-240

Gartner, R, Baker, K and Pampel, FC, 1990, Gender stratification and the gender gap in homicide victimization, *Social Problems*, 37, 4, 593-612

Gibbens, TCN, 1957, Juvenile prostitution, *British Journal of Delinquency*, 8, 1, 3-12

Gibson, DC, 2006, *Serial murder and media circuses*, Westport, CT: Praeger

Goffman, E, 1959, *The presentation of self in everyday life*, New York, NY: Doubleday

Goldstein, J, Freund, A and Solnit, AJ, 1984, *Beyond the best interests of the child* (vol 1), New York, NY: Free Press

Greenwald, H, 1958, *The call girl*, New York, NY: Ballantine Books

Gruenewald, JA and Pridemore, WA, 2009, Stability and change in homicide victim, offender, and event characteristics in Chicago 1900 and 2000, *Homicide Studies*, 13, 4, 355-384

Gurian, EA, 2011, Female serial murderers: directions for future research on a hidden population, *International Journal of Offender Therapy and Comparative Criminology*, 55, 1, 27-42

Hager, T, 2008, Compassion and indifference: the attitude of the English legal system toward Ellen Harper and Selina Wadge, who killed their offspring in the 1870s, *Journal of Family History*, 33, 2, 173-194

Haggerty, KD, 2009, Modern serial killers, *Crime, Media, Culture*, 5, 2, 168-187

Haines, MR, 1977, Fertility, nuptiality and occupation: a study of coal mining populations and regions in England and Wales in the nineteenth century, *Journal of Interdisciplinary History*, 8, 2, 245-280

Hall, M, 1873, Letter to Mary Ann Cotton, March 21, in A Appleton, *Mary Ann Cotton: Her story and trial*, London: Michael Joseph, 124

Hall, VG, 2004, Differing gender roles: women in mining and fishing communities in Northumberland, England 1880-1914, *Women's Studies International Forum*, 27, 5/6, 521-530

Hall, PA and Taylor, RC, 1996, Political science and the three new institutionalisms, *Political Studies*, 44, 5, 936-957

Hall, PA and Taylor, RC, 1996, The potential of historical institutionalism: a response to Hay and Wincott, *Political Studies*, 46, 5, 958-962

Hampton, M, 2004a, *Visions of the press in Britain 1850-1950*, Chicago, IL: University of Illinois Press

Hampton, M, 2004b, Newspapers in Victorian Britain, *History Compass*, 2, 1, 1-8

Harbort, S and Mokros, A, 2001, Serial murderers in Germany from 1945 to 1995: a descriptive study, *Homicide Studies*, 5, 4, 311-334

Harris, J, 2003, *The social work business*, London: Routledge

Harrison, MA, Murphy, EA, Ho, LY, Bowers, TG and Flaherty, CV, 2015, Female serial killers in the United States: means, motives, and makings, *The Journal of Forensic Psychiatry & Psychology*, ahead of print, doi: 10.1080/14789949.2015.1007516

Harvey, D, 2005, *A brief history of neoliberalism*, Oxford: Oxford University Press

Hay, C and Wincott, D, 1998, Structure, agency and historical institutionalism, *Political Studies*, 46, 5, 951-957

Hazelwood, RR and Douglas, JE, 1980, The lust murderer, *FBI Law Enforcement Bulletin*, 49, 18-22

Heidensohn, F, 1968, The deviance of women: a critique and an enquiry, *The British Journal of Sociology*, 19, 2, 160-175

Heidensohn, F, 1981, Women and the penal system, in A Morris and L Gelsthorpe (eds) *Women and crime*, Cambridge: Cropwood

Heidensohn, F, 1985, *Women and crime*, London: Macmillan

Hickey, EW, 1997, *Serial murderers and their victims* (2nd edn), Belmont, CA: Wadsworth

Hickey, EW, 2002, *Serial murderers and their victims* (3rd edn), Belmont, CA: Wadsworth/Thomson Learning

REFERENCES

Hickey, EW, 2006, *Serial murderers and their victims* (4th edn), Belmont, CA: Thompson Wadsworth

Hickey, EW, 2010, *Serial murderers and their victims* (5th edn) Belmont, CA: Thompson Wadsworth.

Hickey, EW, 2012, *Serial murderers and their victims* (6th edn), Belmont, CA: Thompson Wadsworth

Holmes, RM and De Burger, J, 1985, Profiles in terror: the serial murderer, *Federal Probation*, 49, 29-34

Holmes, RM and De Burger, J, 1988, *Serial murder*, Newbury Park, CA: Sage Publications

Holmes, RM and Holmes, ST, 1996, *Profiling violent crimes: An investigative tool*, Thousand Oaks, CA: Sage Publications

Holmes, RM and Holmes, ST, 1994, *Murder in America*, Thousand Oaks, CA: Sage.

Holmes, RM and Holmes, ST (eds), 1998, *Contemporary perspectives on serial murder*, Thousand Oaks, CA: Sage Publications

Holmes, RM and Holmes, ST, 2001, *Murder in America* (2nd edn), Thousand Oaks, CA: Sage Publications

Holmes, RM and Holmes, ST, 2010, *Serial murder* (3rd edn), Los Angeles, CA: Sage Publications

Holmes, ST, Hickey, E and Holmes, RM, 1991, Female serial murderesses: constructing differentiating typologies, *Journal of Contemporary Criminal Justice*, 7, 4, 245-256

Homant, RJ and Kennedy, DB, 2014, Understanding serial sexual murder: a biopsychosocial approach, in W Petherick (ed) *Profiling and serial crime* (3rd edn), Boston, MA: Anderson Publishing, 341-372

Howe, D, 1992, Child abuse and the bureaucratisation of social work, *Sociological Review*, 40, 3, 491-508

Jarvis, B, 2007, Monsters inc.: serial killers and consumer culture, *Crime, Media, Culture*, 3, 3, 326-344

Jenkins, P, 1994, *Using murder: The social construction of serial homicide*, New Brunswick, NJ: Transaction Publishers

Jewkes, Y, 2004, *Media and crime*, London: Sage Publications

Jordan, B, 1998, *The new politics of welfare: Social justice in a global context* (vol 2), London: Sage Publications

Karstedt, S, 2010, New institutionalism in criminology: approaches, theories and theme, in E McLaughlin and T Newburn (eds) *The Sage handbook of criminological theory*, London: Sage Publications, 337-359

Keeney, BT and Heide, KM, 1994, Gender differences in serial murderers: a preliminary analysis, *Journal of Interpersonal Violence*, 9, 3, 37-56

Kelleher, MD and Kelleher, CL, 1998, *Murder most rare: The female serial killer*, Westport, CT: Praeger

Kraemer, GW, Lord, WD and Heilbrun, K, 2004, Comparing single and serial homicide offenses, *Behavioral Sciences and the Law*, 22, 3, 325-343

Kroneberg, C, 2006, The definition of the situation and variable rationality: the model of frame selection as a general theory of action, *Sonderforschungsbereich*, Mannheim, Germany: Mannheim University

Kruttschnitt, C and Carbone-Lopez, K, 2006, Moving beyond the stereotypes: women's subjective accounts of their violent crime, *Criminology*, 44, 2, 321-351

Lacey, N, 2008, *The prisoner's dilemma: Political economy and punishment in contemporary democracies*, Cambridge: Cambridge University Press

LaFree, G, 1998, *Losing legitimacy*, Boulder, CO: Westview

LaFree, G and Drass, KA, 2002, Counting crime booms among nations: evidence for homicide victimization rates 1956-1998, *Criminology*, 40, 4, 769-800

Leonard, EB, 1983, *Women, crime and society*, London: Longmans

Leyton E, 1986, *Hunting humans: The rise of the modern multiple murderer*, Toronto: McClelland & Stewart

Lombroso, C, 1875, *The female offender*, New York, NY: Appleton

Lombroso, C and Ferrero, W, 1885, *The female offender*, London: Unwin

Lowrey, W, 1873, Letter to the Northern Echo, March 19, in A Appleton, *Mary Ann Cotton: Her story and trial*, London: Michael Joseph, 119-120

Maguire, M, 2002, Crime statistics, in M Maguire, R Morgan and R Reiner (eds) *The Oxford handbook of criminology* (2nd edn), Oxford: Oxford University Press, 322-375

REFERENCES

Maher, L, 1997, *Sexed work: Gender, race and resistance in a Brooklyn drug market*, Oxford: Clarendon Press

Mann, CR, 1996, *When women kill*, Albany, NY: State University of New York Press

March, JG and Olsen, JP, 1989, *Rediscovering institutions*, New York, NY: Free Press

March, JG and Olsen, JP, 1998, The institutional dynamics of international political orders, *International Organization*, 52, 4, 943-969

McDonagh, J, 2003, *Child murder and British culture 1720-1900*, Cambridge: Cambridge University Press

McKie, L, 2005, *Families, violence and social change*, Maidenhead: Open University Press

Mead, GH, 1934, *Mind, self and society*, Chicago, IL: University of Chicago Press

Merton, RK, 1964, Anomie, anomia, and social interaction, in B Clinard (ed) *Anomie and deviant behaviour: A discussion and critique*. New York, NY: Free Press, 213-42

Merton, R, 1968, *Social theory and social structure*, New York, NY: Free Press

Messner, SF, 2012, Morality, markets, and the ASC: 2011 presidential address to the American Society of Criminology, *Criminology*, 50, 1, 5-25

Messner, SF and Rosenfeld, RN, 2004, 'Institutionalizing' criminological theory, in J McCord (ed) *Beyond empiricism: Institutions and intentions in the study of crime*, New Brunswick, NJ: Transaction Publishers, 83-106

Messner, SF and Rosenfeld RN, 2007, *Crime and the American dream*, Belmont, CA: Thomson Wadsworth

Messner, SF, Rosenfeld, RN and Karstedt, S, 2013, Social institutions and crime, in FT Cullen and P Wilcox, (eds) *The Oxford handbook of criminological theory*, Oxford: Oxford University Press, 405-423

Metcalfe, A, 2006, *Leisure and recreation in a Victorian mining community: The social economy of leisure in North-East England 1820-1914*, London: Routledge

Meyer, JW and Rowan, B, 1977, Institutionalized organizations: formal structures as myth and ceremony, *American Journal of Sociology*, 83, 2, 340-363

Miles, MB and Huberman, AM, 1994, *Qualitative data analysis* (2nd edn), Thousand Oaks, CA: Sage Publications

Miller, J, 2001, *One of the guys: Girls, gangs and gender*, New York NY: Oxford University Press

Miller, J, 2002, The strengths and limits of 'doing gender' for understanding street crime, *Theoretical Criminology*, 6, 4, 433-460

Miller, J, 2010, Commentary on Heidensohn's 'The deviance of women': continuity and change over four decades of research on gender, crime and social control, *British Journal of Sociology*, 61, 1, 133-139

Morris, AM and Gelsthorpe, LR, 1981, *Women and Crime*, Cropwood Conference Series 13, Cambridge: Institute of Criminology

Morrissey, B, 2003, *When women kill: Questions of agency and subjectivity*, London: Routledge

Morton, RJ and McNamara, JJ, 2005, Serial murder, in J Payne-James (ed) *Encyclopedia of forensic and legal medicine*, Oxford: Elsevier, 47-53

Myers, WC, Gooch, E and Meloy, JR, 2005, The role of psychopathy and sexuality in a female serial killer, *Journal of Forensic Science*, 50, 3, 652-57.

Nivette, A, 2014, Legitimacy and crime: theorizing the role of the state in cross-national criminological theory, *Theoretical Criminology*, 18, 1, 93-111

Nivette, AE and Eisner, M, 2013, Do legitimate polities have fewer homicides? A cross-national analysis, *Homicide Studies*, 17, 1, 3-26

North, DC, 1990, *Institutions, institutional change and economic performance*, Cambridge: Cambridge University Press

Olive, M, 1873, Letter to the Home Secretary, March 24, in A Appleton, *Mary Ann Cotton: Her story and trial*, London: Michael Joseph, 113-114

ONS (Office for National Statistics), 2014, *Crime statistics: Focus on violent crime and sexual offences*, London: ONS

REFERENCES

Orstrosky-Solis, F, Velez-Garcia, A, Santana-Vargas, D, Perez, M and Ardila, A, 2008, A middle-aged female serial killer, *Journal of Forensic Sciences*, 53, 5, 1223-1230

Page, M, 2010, David Cameron's modern conservative approach to poverty and social justice: towards one nation or two?, *Journal of Poverty and Social Justice*, 18, 2, 147-160

Parsons, T, 1959, The social structure of the family, in RN Anshen (ed) *The family: Its functions and destiny*, New York, NY: Harper & Row, 173-201

Payne, G, 2000, *Social divisions*, London: Macmillan

Pearson, P, 1997, *When she was bad: Violent women and the myth of innocence*, New York, NY: Viking

Peters, BG, 1999, *Institutional theory in political science: The 'new' institutionalisms*, New York, NY: Pinter

Phelps, MW, 2011, *Devil's rooming house: The true story of America's deadliest female serial killer*, Guilford, CT: Lyons Press

Pollak, O, 1961, *The criminality of women*, New York, NY: A.S. Barnes

Potter, H, 2006, An argument for black feminist criminology: understanding African American women's experiences with intimate partner violence using an integrated approach, *Feminist Criminology*, 1, 2, 106-124

Powell, WW and DiMaggio, PJ, 1991, *The new institutionalism in organizational analysis*, Chicago, IL: University of Chicago Press

Pridemore, WA, 2007, Change and stability in the characteristics of homicide victims, offenders and incidents during rapid social change, *British Journal of Criminology*, 47, 2, 331-345

Pridemore, WA and Kim, S, 2007, Socioeconomic change and homicide in transnational society, *The Sociological Quarterly*, 48, 2, 229-251

Quinet, K, 2007, The missing missing: toward a quantification of serial murder victimization in the United States, *Homicide Studies*, 11, 4, 319-339

R v Mariusz Krezolek and Magdalena Łuczak, 2013, Sentencing remarks of Mrs Justice Cox, 2 August, Birmingham Crown Court

Rappaport, RG, 1988, The serial and mass murderer, *American Journal of Forensic Psychiatry*, 9, 1, 39-48

Ressler, RK, Burgess, AW and Douglas, JE, 1988, *Sexual homicide: Patterns and motives*, New York, NY: Free Press

Ressler, RK, Burgess, AW, Douglas, JE, Hartman, CR and D'Agostino, RB, 1986, Serial killers and their victims: identifying patterns through crime scene analysis, *International Journal of Violence*, 1, 3, 288–308

Reynolds, M, 2004, *Dead ends: The pursuit, conviction and execution of female serial killer Aileen Wuornos, the damsel of death*, New York, NY: St Martin's Paperbacks

Rogowski, S, 2012, Social work with children and families: challenges and possibilities in the neo-liberal world, *British Journal of Social Work*, 42, 5, 921-940

Rose, L, 1986, *The massacre of the innocents: Infanticide in Britain 1800-1939*, London: Routledge & Kegan Paul

Rose, SO, 1992, *Limited livelihoods: Gender and class in nineteenth century England*, Berkeley, CA: University of California Press

Rosenfeld, RN, 2011, The big picture: 2010 presidential address to the American Society of Criminology, *Criminology*, 49, 1, 1-26

Rosenfeld, RN and Messner, SF, 2011, The intellectual origins of institutional anomie theory, in FT Cullen, CL Jonson, AJ Myer and F Adler (eds) *The origins of American criminology*, New Brunswick, NJ: Transaction, 121-135

Rosenfeld, R and Messner, SF, 2013, *Crime and the economy*, London: Sage Publications

Roth, R, 2009, *American homicide*, Cambridge, MA: Harvard University Press

Rowbotham, S, 1977, *Hidden from history: 300 years of women's oppression and the fight against it*, London: Pluto

Santtila, P, Pakkanen, T, Zappala, A, Bosco, D, Valkama, M and Mokros, A, 2008, Behavioural crime linking in serial homicide, *Psychology, Crime and Law*, 14, 3, 245-265

Schechter, H, 2003, *Fatal: The poisonous life of a female serial killer*, New York, NY: Simon & Schuster

Schmidt, D, 2005, *Natural born celebrities: Serial killers in American culture*, Chicago, IL: University of Chicago Press

Schurman-Kauflin, D, 2000, *The new predator: Women who kill*, New York, NY: Algora Publishing

Scott, H, 2005, The 'gentler sex': patterns in female serial murder, in RN Kocsis (ed) *Serial murder and the psychology of violent crimes*, Totowa, NJ: Humana Press, 179-196

Seal, L, 2010, *Women, murder and femininity: Gender representations of women who kill*, Basingstoke: Palgrave Macmillan

Sharp, SF and Hefley, K, 2007, This is a man's world…or at least that's how it looks in the journals, *Critical Criminology*, 15, 3, 3-18

Shaw, C, 1930, *The jack-roller: A delinquent boy's own story*, Chicago, IL: University of Chicago Press

Silvio, H, McCloskey, K and Ramos-Grenier, J, 2006, Theoretical consideration of female sexual predator serial killers in the United States, *Journal of Criminal Justice*, 34, 3, 251-259

Simons, H, 2009, *Case study research in practice*, London: Sage Publications

Skrapec, CA, 2001, Defining serial murder: a call for a return to the original Lustmörd, *Journal of Police and Criminal Psychology*, 16, 2, 10-24

Smart, C, 1976, *Women, crime and criminology: A feminist critique*, London: Routledge & Kegan Paul

Smart, C, 1996, Deconstructing motherhood in EB Silva, ed, *Good enough mothering? Feminist perspectives on lone mothering*, London: Routledge, pp 37-57.

Smith, RL and Valenze, DM, 1988, Mutuality and marginality: liberal moral theory and working class women in nineteenth century England, *Signs: Journal of Women in Culture and Society*, 13, 2, 277-298

Soothill, K, 2001, The Harold Shipman case: a sociological perspective, *The Journal of Forensic Psychiatry*, 12, 2, 260-262

Soothill, K and Wilson, D, 2005, Theorising the puzzle that is Harold Shipman, *Journal of Forensic Psychiatry and Psychology*, 16, 4, 658-98

Spencer, H, 1851, *Social statics*, Milton Keynes: Lightning Source, 2012

Stamatel, JP, 2014, Explaining variations in female homicide victimization rates across Europe. *European Journal of Criminology*, 11, 5, 578-600

Thelen, K, 1999, Historical institutionalism in comparative politics, *Annual Review of Political Science*, 2, 1, 369-404

Thompson, H, 1976, *Durham villages*, London: Robert Hale

Thompson, J and Ricard, S, 2009, Women's role in serial killing teams: reconstructing a radical feminist perspective, *Critical Criminology*, 17, 4, 261-275

Timmins, N, 1995, *The five giants*, London: Fontana

Tulloch, J, 2006, The privatising of pain: Lincoln newspapers 'mediated publicness' and the end of the public execution, *Journalism Studies*, 7, 3, 437-451

Walker, A, 2006, The development of the provincial press in England c. 1780-1914, *Journalism Studies*, 7, 3, 373-386

Walklate, S, 2003, *Understanding criminology: Current theoretical debates*, Buckingham: Open University Press

Way, LB, 2004, Missing faces: is historical institutionalism the answer for conducting intersectional research?, *Women and Criminal Justice*, 15, 2, 81-98

Wesley, JK, 2006, Considering the context of women's violence: gender, lived experiences and cumulative victimization, *Feminist Criminology*, 1, 4, 303-328

West, C and Zimmerman, DH, 1987, Doing gender, *Gender and Society*, 1, 2, 125-151

White, J and Lester, D, 2012, A study of female serial killers, *American Journal of Forensic Psychology*, 30, 1, 25-29

Whitehead, T, 2000, *Mary Ann Cotton: Dead but not forgotten*, Seaham: Tony Whitehead

Wiener, MJ, 2007, Convicted murderers and the Victorian Press: condemnation versus sympathy, *Crimes and Misdemeanours*, 1, 2, 110-125

Wilkinson, R and Pickett, K, 2010, *The spirit level: Why equality is better for everyone*, London: Penguin

Wilson, D, 2007, *Serial killers: Hunting Britons and their victims, 1960-2006*, Winchester: Waterside Press

Wilson, D, 2009, *A history of British serial killing 1888-2008*, London: Sphere

REFERENCES

Wilson, D, 2013, *Mary Ann Cotton: Britain's first serial killer*, Winchester: Waterside

Wilson, D and Yardley, E, 2013, The psychopathy of a Victorian serial killer: integrating micro and macro levels of analysis, *Journal of Criminal Psychology*, 3, 1, 19-30

Wilson, D, Yardley, E and Lynes, A, 2015, *Serial killers and the phenomenon of serial murder*, Winchester: Waterside

Wilson, W and Hilton, T, 1998, Modus operandi of female serial killers, *Psychological Reports*, 82, 2, 495-498

Yin, RK, 2009, *Case study research: Design and methods*, Thousand Oaks, CA: Sage Publications

Newspaper articles

Newcastle Courant, 14 March 1873, Female poisoners, 3

Newcastle Courant, 14 March 1873, The West Auckland poisoner, 5

The Leeds Mercury, 8 March 1873, Nobody can wish to deal harshly, 7

The Leeds Mercury, 20 March 1873, The condemned convict Mary Ann Cotton, 8

The London Standard, 10 March 1873, The most noteworthy incident of the present Lent Assizes, 5

The Newcastle Daily Journal, 11 March 1873, The West Auckland poisonings, 6

The Northern Echo, 6 March 1873, Durham Spring Assizes – Wednesday, 3-4

The Northern Echo, 8 March 1873, Durham Spring Assizes – Friday, 3-4

The Northern Echo, 15 March 1873, Mary Anne Cotton in Durham jail, 3

The Northern Echo, 22 March 1873, The West Auckland poisonings: the baby at West Auckland, 3

The Northern Echo, 24 March 1873, The West Auckland poisonings: affecting interview with her stepfather, 3

The Northern Echo, 25 March 1873, The West Auckland poisonings: prisoner in the condemned cell, 3

The Northern Echo, 28 March 1873, Mrs Cotton's farewell to her friends and baby, 3

INDEX